My
My Wri

A Memoir

Iola Mathews

My Mother,
My Writing and Me

A Memoir

Iola Mathews

M
A   MICHELLE ANDERSON PUBLISHING

MELBOURNE

First published in Australia 2009
by Michelle Anderson Publishing Pty Ltd
PO Box 6032
Chapel Street North
South Yarra 3141
Melbourne Australia
Email: mapubl@bigpond.net.au
Website: www.michelleandersonpublishing.com

Cover design: Luke Harris, Chameleon Print Design
Typeset by Midland Typesetters, Australia
Printed by McPherson's Printing Group, Australia

National Library of Australia cataloguing-in-publication data

Author: Mathews, Iola

Title: My mother, my writing and me / Iola Mathews

ISBN: 978085572 (pbk.)

Subjects: Mathews, Iola.
            Baby boom generation—Australia—Biography.
            Baby boom generation—Australia—Attitudes.
            Middle aged women—Australia—Biography.
            Interpersonal relations—Australia
            Intergenerational relations—Australia.
            Australia—Social conditions—2001 –

Dewey Number: 305.20994.

*The events described in this book are true; however a few names have been
changed to preserve the privacy of individuals.*

Contents

Acknowledgements

This book would not have been written without the help and encouragement of many people. I wish to thank Dr Peter O'Connor for his wise counsel when I was 'blocked' and Barbara Turner-Vesselago whose writing course Freefall (www.freefallwriting.com) showed me a new way of writing.

I would like to thank those who read this book in draft form and gave me detailed feedback – in particular Selena de Lang, Fiona Wood, Joan Grant, Jackie Yowell, Sheila Drummond and my daughter Talya Mathews.

I would like to thank the National Trust of Australia (Victoria) for allowing me to have a room at Glenfern in East St Kilda and to work with them to establish the writers' studios there. That project would not have gone ahead without the support of Joel Becker, director of the Victorian Writers' Centre (www.vwc.org.au) and the funding bodies which made it possible, in particular the Victorian Government and the Pratt Foundation.

I would like to thank my publisher Michelle Anderson for understanding so quickly what this book was about and her ongoing support (www.michelleandersonpublishing. com.)

Finally, I would like to thank my family for allowing me to write about them in such a personal way – my brother, my sister, my step-children, my children and my husband Race Mathews whose love and encouragement have sustained me through thirty-six years of marriage.

Iola Mathews, 2009

Prologue

'Midway this way of life we're bound upon,
I woke to find myself in a dark wood
Whence the right road was wholly lost and gone.'

And so begins *The Divine Comedy* by Dante Alighieri. The poet descends into Hell and faces some demons, but guided by Virgil, eventually finds his way back to earth, *'to look once more upon the stars'*. This epic poem is an allegory for a spiritual journey.

At forty, approaching mid-life, I found myself in a dark wood of my own after my career as a journalist came unexpectedly to an end. I had been in journalism since my twenties and loved it with a passion. It enabled me to pursue two of the things I cared about most, writing and social justice. It took me a year to find another job. In that period I discovered the meaning of the words 'mid life crisis'. You realise with a shock that instead of your life being all in front of you, at least half of it is now behind you. The realisation can be painful, but once you pass through it you have renewed enjoyment for life.

For some of us, there is another dark wood in the fifties, when we make the transition from the busy world of the forties (work, children, mortgage, responsibilities, no time for yourself) to the sixties, and the quieter world of retirement. For most people, the fifties is the decade when your children leave home, your financial pressures and responsibilities are not so extreme and you have more time to enjoy life. But it can also be the time when your career path peaks, your body starts to sag, and you wonder how you will fill in the days when you retire. You sometimes turn away from the busy outer world towards the inner world of reflection.

In my late fifties I found myself once again in confusion. I wanted to give up my job in the corporate world and return to writing, but I had 'writer's block'. I wanted time for myself, but I was increasingly busy helping my elderly mother who was unwell. As I watched her go downhill I had to face up to her mortality and my own. I felt myself once more lost in a 'dark wood' until I was guided out of it with the help of a book called *Facing the Fifties*, a creative writing course and the joy of becoming a grandmother. By the time I turned sixty I had regained peace and happiness and could 'look once more upon the stars'.

This is the story of that journey.

1

Trapped

'I was fifty-eight and my life was stalled, like a train carriage shunted into a siding.'

On a cool morning in early September, I sat by my mother's hospital bed and watched her sleep. Her mouth was slightly open, her white hair brushed back on the pillow. She lay on her side, facing me, one hand under the pillow, the other resting on the crisp white sheet. She stirred and I thought she'd wake, but instead she coughed a little and swallowed dryly before she relaxed again into sleep. Thank God she's not in pain, I thought, and settled back into the comfortable chair between the bed and the window. It was nice to take a moment out of my busy life to sit and think.

I gazed out the window. We were on the second floor of a private hospital, looking down on a small roundabout in East Melbourne. Inside the room it was warm and quiet, but through the window I could see the cold wind fluttering the umbrellas outside the cafe across the road. A man and a woman in overcoats sat under the umbrellas, talking, with mobile phones beside their coffee cups. A man on a bicycle rode past, pushing into the wind.

I looked at my mother's thin arms, black with bruises from her recent fall, the veins standing out thickly. I felt a sudden rush of love for her and took hold of her hand, a tiny bundle of bones; warm as a little bird. The skin was bruised, the fingers gnarled, but the nails were still long and freshly painted, bright red. 'All the nurses admire my long nails,' she had said proudly the day before. 'I keep them long so people will look at them instead of my horrible hands.'

While I held her hand, marvelling at its softness, she stirred, opened her eyes and gave me a big smile. 'How lovely to see you,' she said. 'How long have you been here?'

'Not long. I didn't want to wake you. How do you feel?'

She thought about this and then said, 'Thirsty.'

'I have something for you.' I reached into my bag.

'What's that?'

'A special cup,' I said, not telling her it was for a baby. I showed her the spout from which she could drink. I had noticed the day before that her shaky hands could not hold a cup or glass without spilling it. I filled the baby cup with water and helped her to sit up a little, then supported her back and raised the cup to her lips.

She took a few sips and said, 'Ah, that's better.' She handed me the cup and lay down again. Then, after a few minutes, 'I need to go to the toilet, will you help me?'

'What about the nurse?'

'They take ages to come. You can help me, can't you?'

'Of course.' I went to the end of the bed and brought up her walking frame. Then I pulled back the blankets and slowly helped her up until she was sitting on the edge of the bed. She breathed deeply, steadying herself from the effort. I put her slippers on her feet and straightened the bed-jacket which had ridden up her back. As I leant over, I smelt the musty smell of her hair and a faint ammonia scent of urine. I put the walking frame in front of her and placed her hands on the handles.

'Try to stand up, Mum,' I said, and watched her get shakily to her feet. She stood, leaning on the handles for a minute and then made her way very slowly into the bathroom. I held the door open while she went in and watched her turn around until she was standing in front of the toilet. She slowly lifted her nightdress, and I saw that she was wearing a large disposable nappy.

'Let me help you,' I said, and she stood obediently while I undid the plastic strips holding the nappy together and let it drop, damply, to the floor. Then I helped her to sit down. I put the nappy in the disposal bin and found a fresh one in the drawer by her bed and brought it back to the bathroom, ready for when she needed it.

'I'll be here a while,' she said. 'Wait outside and I'll call you when I'm ready.'

I went back to the chair by the window. A young mother with a pram stood on the pavement below, chatting to an older woman. The wind whipped the trees and blew some leaves into the gutter.

I thought about my mother and how I had helped my children in the same way when they were very small. So much was the same – their helplessness, their dependency, and the slow speed of everything. If you tried to hurry them, you only got frustrated. You had to summon up reserves of patience and slow down to their pace.

I had a flashback to a time, a dozen years earlier, when I took a week off work to mind my three year old step grand-daughter Cosima, while her mother was in hospital having her second child. Each day I would take Cosima to a bakery nearby to get fresh rolls for lunch. The walk to the bakery would take an adult a brisk ten minutes, but at Cosima's pace it took perhaps forty minutes.

She would start off holding my hand and skipping along the footpath. Then she would stop to examine a piece of paper on the ground, squatting on her haunches, delicately picking it up and turning it over. Next, she would stop to peer through a fence at a cat in someone's garden. Talking to the cat and looking at the garden might take up ten minutes. Then we would start again until something else distracted her. This stop-start progress was accompanied by a continuous commentary from her. During that week, I slowed down to her pace and saw the world through her eyes. It was so different from my busy office life.

Now I was doing it again. No point rushing into the hospital and saying I had only twenty minutes. That would barely give my mother time to sit up. Better to give up two hours and forget the world outside. Better to adjust to her rhythm. I took my mobile phone out of my handbag and turned it off. The office could wait.

A small voice from the bathroom interrupted my thoughts. 'Are you there, dear?'

I jumped up. She was still sitting on the toilet. 'I'm in a spot of bother,' she said. 'I think there's a bit of a mess.' I bent over her and lifted her nightdress and saw that she'd soiled it and was too weak to clean it up herself. I wrinkled my nose and said 'oh, yuk' to myself. I took the toilet paper and wiped her, then cleaned her with a damp cloth and dried her with a towel.

'We'd better change your nightie,' I said.

'Oh dear, I should have got the nurse, shouldn't I?'

I didn't answer. You never knew how long the nurses would take after you rang the bell. It was quicker to do it yourself. I fetched a clean nightdress and helped take off her clothes. She stood naked and helpless, her body skin and bone, the flesh hanging off her buttocks in folds. I dressed her again, then propped her against me while I struggled to put a clean disposable nappy between her legs. Trying to hold her up and fasten the nappy was a struggle. She tried to help and then started to giggle. I stopped and giggled with her and we clung together for a moment, laughing weakly.

'Oh, God, it's awful being old,' my mother said. 'I don't know what I'd do without you.'

'Well you used to do all this for me when I was little, so it's only fair that I help you now, isn't it?' I said in my cheerful, hospital-visiting voice, not wanting her to see my pity at such helplessness. She held up the nightdress while I fastened the nappy. Then I let the nightdress drop, put on her bedjacket and led her to the basin so she could wash her hands.

A nurse appeared in the doorway, large and buxom. 'You should have called me,' she said rather crossly, and then to my mother: 'I'll help you.'

Back in bed, my mother lay on the pillow, exhausted. 'Why don't you have a sleep now,' I said. 'I'll read for a while.' She nodded and whispered, 'Thank you darling.'

I opened my book but did not read. I thought about lunch-time. I would feed her again. The day before, I had found her trying to eat her lunch, but her hands were too weak to hold the knife and fork properly or to cut the meat and the nurses were too busy to help her.

'Here she is,' I thought, 'just like a baby.' I thought about birth and death, two of the great mysteries of life. My father had died five years earlier. My mother was ninety-four-and-a-half and lived in a retirement home. She had been in and out of different hospitals for months, mainly for falls. Each time there had been a slow recovery and a peaceful period before the next fall, but each one had left her a bit weaker, like a downwards escalator. I had watched her shrinking in size as her shoulders became more stooped and her flesh sagged like a wrinkled cloth. I had sat by her bed and held her hand and thought about the long sweep of her life, nearly a century in all.

Throughout her life she'd always been so alive, so beautiful and competent, quick and smiling. She was the one who looked after everyone else. Now it was her turn to be looked after. I wondered who would look after me when I became old. Did I want my children to go through all this? I looked out the window and watched the wind whipping a piece of rubbish along the pavement and thought about my current predicament.

I was fifty-eight and my life was stalled, like a train carriage shunted into a siding. I had reduced my paid work to three days a week in order to have time to write, but my writing was going nowhere. Most of the time I was too busy looking after my mother, and on the rare occasions that I had free time, I wrestled with writer's block.

Sometimes I thought I should give up work altogether. Other days I thought I should look for another job, a new challenge. But for how long would my mother need me? It could be years. There was no escape, for her or for me.

I thought about how well she had been until a year earlier. Until then, she'd fooled everyone by looking much younger than her age. She had been a merry widow, with a cosy room in a retirement home. She treated it like a luxury hotel, coming and going in her little car to bridge, shopping or to my place for dinner.

On her ninety-third birthday, my husband and I took her to a jazz club. She'd been a 'flapper' in the 1920s and taught my brother and sister and me all the old jazz songs. When we were teenagers she showed all our friends how to do the charleston. So as soon as we entered the jazz club she was in her element, smiling and tapping her feet, her blue eyes darting around.

Shortly after we arrived, a man with white hair and white shoes asked her to dance. She was thrilled, and spent most of the night dancing with him. He was in his seventies and thought she was too. She did not disillusion him. At some point he asked me to dance with him instead, and held me too close. I tried to push him away, and when the dance finished he said, 'your mother's a wonderful dancer, you know, she's better than you are.'

'I know she is,' I said, laughing, and rushed back to tell Mum. Driving her home later, she giggled and told us that the man with the white shoes had asked her to go with him to a jazz festival in New South Wales, on a bus with some other people. She told him coyly that she'd think about it. She couldn't wait to tell her friends in the retirement home, and danced down the corridor to her room when we dropped her off. I marvelled at her skill in giving men the brush-off. My father once said that she could say no to a man and still make him feel good. I asked her how she did it and she said, 'With a smile.'

A few months after the jazz club, when Mum was still well, the Queen Mother turned one hundred. The retirement home organised a special party, and asked Mum to appear as the Queen Mother. She loved it. She wore a tiara and long white gloves and waved her hand regally as she entered the dining room. She put on a fake royal accent and gave a little speech. She said,

When my dear husband took the throne in 1936 and I became his Queen, I had no idea that I would still be here for the millennium, but here I am. The world has changed very much since then. I have enjoyed my life to the full, even with the inevitable ups and downs. We have seen astronauts walking on the moon, the atom has been split, the huge oceans have been sailed by lone seamen and the tallest mountains have been conquered. Truly I have lived in a wonderful era. Thank you for inviting me to take tea with you today.

The speech had echoes of Mum's own life, which had also spanned the twentieth century. When she showed it to me I noted that she did not mention the two world wars or the Depression, although she'd lived through those too. She always focused on the positive.

Shortly after her triumph as the Queen Mother, she had a small stroke which affected her left arm. She was in the dining room when it happened and the staff immediately called the doctor. He said it was a TIA, *a transient ischemic attack*. It only lasted twenty-four hours and then she was leading her busy life again, joining in all the activities in the retirement home – carpet bowls, mahjong, exercises, dancing, bridge and drinks before dinner with her friends. She was popular and loved the communal life, just as she had loved boarding school eighty years earlier.

A few months later she developed a kidney disease and went into hospital to have one of her kidneys removed. The doctor said the disease was caused by amyloid deposits, a condition which could come out of the blue with elderly people. He said she would function perfectly well with one kidney, and she did.

Mum turned ninety-four and shortly afterwards had another TIA. She fell in her bathroom and was bruised all over. The doctor told her to rest, but the following day she got out of bed and somehow pulled the television down on top of her and cut her leg. She said she was trying to move the TV because the rug underneath was not in the right place. When the manager of the retirement home rang to tell me what had happened I was horrified, but then it occurred to me that it was typical of her, always the perfect housewife. The cut was so deep she went into hospital for a skin graft, and after that, was supposed to use a walking frame. Sometimes she did, but at other times she found it a nuisance, and tried to walk without it.

And so here I was, sitting by her hospital bed again. This time she had fallen during the night when she was on her way to the toilet, without her walking frame. The staff went into her room to wake her for breakfast at eight a.m. and discovered her on the floor, unable to remember how she got there. There were no cuts or bruises, but her face was red and swollen from lying in a pool of urine and she was very confused. She was in hospital now for a rest and for observation. I leaned over and looked closely at her face. It had a few red scratches on the cheek but the swelling had gone down. I hoped that in a few days, she would be able to go home.

The next day my mother was feeling better and she was able to get up and walk around the ward and watch tele-vision. The following day I had to go to work, but rushed over to the hospital in my lunch hour. When I arrived she was sitting up in bed, waiting. 'Where have you been?' she said crossly. 'I tried to phone you at home but you weren't there. I thought you were going to come in this morning and tell me about the doctor and the x-rays.'

I immediately felt irritated. 'I said I'd come in sometime today, Mum, I didn't say this morning,' I said. 'I'm at work today and I can't stay long.'

She looked anxious. 'When you didn't answer the phone, I thought, what do I do now? You're the only person left that I've got. Who else can I contact?'

'You could ring the retirement home,' I said, but she didn't reply. I was 'it' and we both knew it and it was my burden.

I sat down and said, 'I phoned the doctor this morning. He says the x-rays are clear. There's nothing broken and there's no infection, but he'd like to keep you in a few more days.' I didn't tell her I thought this was unnecessary and wondered if the doctor had shares in the hospital and wanted to keep the beds full. Instead I said, 'When he comes to see you, why don't you tell him you'd like to go home sooner? I could take you home tomorrow if you feel up to it.' I hoped she'd say yes, because the staff in the retirement home looked after her well, and I wouldn't have to visit every day.

She looked surprised. 'But I've only been in a couple of days and I'm not ready to see everybody yet. Can you give me a mirror?' I rummaged in my handbag and passed her my powder compact. She scrutinised her face and said, 'I look a fright. I'd like to stay a bit longer until my face clears up.' I stared at her and thought crossly, 'It's just vanity. Great! Let her stay a week! Why should I worry about everything, even the bloody health budget?' I was about to say something when the nurse entered the room with a tray and said she was going to help Mum with her lunch. I leapt up and said goodbye and rushed out, feeling guilty.

As I caught a tram back to work I thought, *when she's better I'll tell her about Queenscliff.* I had booked to go to a creative writing course in three weeks' time. It was a residential course and I'd be away for a week. She wouldn't like that. I was her sole support, since my brother lived on the other side of the world and my sister lived in northern NSW and was mostly too unwell to visit.

Suddenly I felt angry at being the only one looking after Mum. There's always one sucker who looks after the elderly parents, I thought sourly, while the others nick off. What if I just went away like them and left her all alone, how would they like that? But my anger towards my brother and sister quickly evaporated. I knew they felt guilty about leaving it all to me and they were good at keeping in touch. I'd always been the dutiful one and I was used to it. I liked helping people. I just wanted time for myself as well. *Please don't fall over again,* I thought, *I really want to go to this course.*

My thoughts switched to the other piece of information I was hiding from her. My twenty-six year old daughter, Talya, was expecting a baby. I had six step-grandchildren and they had given me great pleasure, but this one was different, not least because Talya was going to be a single parent and would need my help more than the others. She'd been living in Japan for some years and now she was coming home, in time for Christmas. I hadn't told my mother about this yet, because I knew she wouldn't approve.

I thought about this new baby and about Talya's birth twenty-six years earlier. I remembered Talya leaving home in her twenties and living overseas, as I had done. I thought about the mother-daughter bond and about the cycle of life ending and renewing itself.

I felt excited about the new baby, but at the same time I was worried. How would Talya manage as a single parent? Would the baby's father be involved? Would the baby bring Talya and me closer again, or would she be distant, as she had been a lot of the time in recent years? I wondered if she would be expecting me to help mind the baby, and I felt a knot tighten inside my stomach.

I thought about my mother and wondered how long it would be before she had another fall. How long did she have to live? Would it be months or years? When she was in hospital my life was put on hold. With the new baby as well, would I have time for myself and my writing? I felt trapped.

2

Facing the Fifties

'Increasingly I felt a desire to write something about my life, to make sense of it all. I started scribbling down ideas and stories from the past and filing them in folders, one for each decade.'

W anting to write was not a pastime to fill in my later years, it was an obsession. I couldn't exist without it. Putting words on paper was like eating and drinking to me, and sometimes even more important. I'd been a journalist in my early life, but then changed career. Now I wanted to return to writing, but I was struggling with the *what* and the *how*. At fifty-eight, I was full of doubt and confusion, and found myself looking back over my life, trying to understand where I'd come from and where I should go next.

Why does someone become a writer? In my case, it was bound up with a love of reading, a delight in the feeling of pen on paper, and in learning to be a quiet observer of the world around me. I also wanted passionately to understand things and to make a difference. These were the things that shaped my life and choice of career, although

I often veered off course like a bird with a broken wing, and crashed around in desperation before I found my way again.

As a child I read a lot, but there was no encouragement for creative writing, at home or at school. The first time I glimpsed the possibility of writing differently was when I was about twelve and joined the local Girl Guide troop. As a guide, you had to pass various tests in order to win badges for your uniform. I struggled to learn knots and semaphore, but when I heard there was a badge for writing, I put up my hand immediately. I was told to take a pencil and notepad and sit somewhere for half an hour and record what I could see, hear, smell, taste and feel.

When I got home, I went outside the back door of our house and sat on the concrete steps and scribbled everything down. I was amazed at how much was going on that I hadn't noticed properly before. I could hear the sound of the train pulling in beside our house, the guard blowing his whistle, people talking on the platform, a bird calling in the oak tree, a plane passing overhead, my mother singing in the laundry next to me. I could smell the sour odour of the gully trap next to the steps and the freshness of the grass. I walked down to the trellis to smell the sweetness of the roses and felt the springiness of the grass under my bare feet and the wet tongue of our Labrador as he licked my hand. The sun was on my face and the sky was a clear blue.

I could have written for hours. I was in the garden I loved, alone with my thoughts, entering deeply into the moment by noticing everything in detail. It was a moment of pure happiness, but it would be another decade before

I started seeing things that way again and writing about them.

In my early twenties I left Australia and started travelling. Suddenly my senses were on full alert again. I wrote long letters every week to my parents describing all the places I'd seen, the people I'd met and the strange or funny things that happened along the way. Then I moved to Paris to live and started to keep a journal. I tried to write fiction, but I thought it was no good and eventually abandoned it. In those days there were no creative writing courses to help, or none that I was aware of anyway.

When I returned to Australia at the age of twenty-six, I was determined to become a journalist. After knocking on doors repeatedly I finally made it, and then everything fell into place. I used to sit at my desk at 'The Age' and marvel that I was being paid for doing something that made me so happy. I loved the research, I loved interviewing people and I enjoyed the challenge of putting the right words on paper. I loved the excitement and the adrenalin and the camaraderie. I was finding out new things every single day – no story was the same.

I learned to write news stories and interviews and feature articles. I wrote on education for some years and helped to start a new supplement called Education Age. After I married and had children, I worked part-time and wrote on a broader range of topics, as well as the things that preoccupied me at the time, the so-called 'women's issues.' I started to write more about people's feelings and occasionally, some personal pieces.

Journalism enabled me to combine the things I loved – researching, writing and finding things out. People go into journalism for different reasons. Some love the thrill of the chase and become investigative reporters or war correspondents. Some like to write poetically and some like to write with humour. I was one of those who liked the idea that journalism could 'shed light in dark corners.'

During this time I also published a book about the news media, demystifying it for community groups and individuals. The book sold well and was reprinted three times by three different publishers. I felt thrilled that I was now an author as well as a journalist.

In the early 1980s, when my children were settled into school, I started to think about taking on more responsibility at work. But it was not a good time to do so. The paper was at the time male-dominated and the management was fairly conservative. I asked if I could write feature articles or leaders (editorials) but was not encouraged. Some of my female colleagues were also rebuffed for senior jobs. We drank coffee together and bitched about management. We noted that although the chief political correspondent was a woman, there were no female leader writers or female foreign correspondents. There were no female heads of editorial sections, except for the women's pages and an entertainment magazine.

I had been part of the women's movement since the early seventies, and was alert to discrimination, but we didn't know how to complain without jeopardising our jobs. Equal opportunity policies were not yet in vogue. I was relegated to a 'lifestyle' section and when I wrote a long feature article on child care, it was rejected. I felt a growing anger and frustration. Some of my female colleagues left and I wondered if I should too.

Then one day in 1982 it all came to a head. There was a state election and Labor won. My husband, Race Mathews, was a backbencher and now became a Minister in the new Government. I knew that the editor of my newspaper would see this as a problem. Ten years earlier, when I was Education writer for the newspaper and Race was an MP in the federal parliament, I had been accused of political bias by a conservative politician when I wrote about problems in the state education system. The editor of the day defended me robustly in the newspaper, saying the comments were 'contemptible' and 'Mrs Mathews has our confidence.' But now things were different. That editor was no longer alive, and I did not believe the current editor would want such a fight.

I could see no way forward, so I went into the editor's office and resigned. He said he understood why, and that he had already decided that I would have to stay away from sensitive areas and policy issues. He suggested that perhaps I could do some kind of research, like checking things for the sub-editors. I felt shocked and powerless. If he'd offered to defend me, I was sure I could have written on serious subjects without bias. But that was not going to happen. My career in journalism was over and I felt sick about it.

As I walked to the lift, one of my colleagues congratulated me on Race's appointment. I mumbled something about having resigned and he said, 'I thought you would, because you'll have such a busy and exciting life now helping your husband.' I looked at him in despair. Bloody stupid men, I thought, can't they see that I have a career too, and now it's in tatters? Do they think I'd be happy trailing after my husband all day, wearing a hat and gloves? I fled the building in tears.

I was thirty-nine. I applied for jobs outside journalism but was rejected for lack of experience. I struggled with a mid-life crisis and it took me a year to get another job. I started researching Affirmative Action policies and ended up working in the Victorian public service, but after twelve months I had to resign. Once more, it was because of my husband's position.

But just when things were at their worst, I had a lucky break. Bill Kelty, Secretary of the Australian Council for Trade Unions, invited me to take up a position implementing a new program on women's employment. I took the job and loved it. Then after a few years I became an industrial officer and advocate, running national test cases on wages and conditions and finally, worked on a national task force on regional economic development. I spent ten years at the ACTU and it was an exciting time, the peak of my 'professional' life.

It was the period of the 'Accord' between the Federal Government and the ACTU, a time when everything seemed possible. I was part of a small team of ACTU staff who had access to government ministers and their departments. We were involved in government policy-making and decisions. We represented Australia overseas, made speeches and hosted conferences.

I learned how to operate in the world of unions and politics and I loved it. During that time my writing skills were used in producing factual material. But at night I kept my journal going and at work I often felt like a fly on the wall, taking it all in, recording what I'd seen.

But in my middle fifties I found myself once again at a crossroads. I had left the ACTU and moved into the corporate sector, working in venture capital, liaising with the union superannuation funds. My working life had zigzagged all over the place by now, and my step-son jokingly said my career could only be explained by 'chaos theory.' I laughed at that, but the truth was simpler. I had moved from one project to another as I followed what interested me at the time. The corporate job was exciting at first, meeting new people and learning new things, but after a few years it was no longer fulfilling. I cut back my job to three days a week and wondered what to do next.

I felt a strong tug back to writing, but I was not sure in what direction. I'd been out of journalism too long to return there. Increasingly I felt a desire to write something about my life, to make sense of it all. I started scribbling down ideas and stories from the past and filing them in folders, one for each decade.

I gave up reading fiction and concentrated on biographies and autobiographies. I wanted to see how other people lived their lives and how they reflected on them. I read dozens of memoirs and made notes. There seemed to be many different approaches. I particularly liked the clarity and honesty of *Personal History*, by Katharine Graham, publisher of *The Washington Post*. I was gripped by *Are You Somebody?* by the Irish journalist Nuala O'Faolain, and the small, perfect memoir by Raymond Gaita, *Romulus, My Father*. I loved anything that made me laugh, like Clive James' *Unreliable Memoirs* about his childhood in Sydney.

I went back to some of my favourite memoir writers, to

George Orwell, Arthur Koestler, Simone de Beavoir, Vera Brittain and Beatrice Webb. I liked the way they had successfully combined writing with political activism. When I was younger, they had inspired me. Now I could see more clearly their faults as well as their successes, because they were first and foremost writers, and were prepared to reveal themselves fully.

When I looked back on my life, I saw two threads bobbing up and down like coloured strands of wool. One was the 'outer' life with all the different jobs and experiences, rich and varied. The other was the 'inner' life where so much had gone on, but was hidden. I did not feel ready to stand naked on the page, like my heroes. How could I write about my childhood without revealing the problems under the surface of my respectable, middle class family? How could I write about my adult life and the ups and downs of my marriage, my stepchildren and my children?

Could I write about the wonderful counsellors who had rescued me from various disasters and taught me wisdom and strength? I could not imagine making any of this public, yet I was drawn totally to the idea of putting it all on paper. That's what writers do. They're compulsive. I could write it for myself and put it in a bottom drawer, but like all writers I wanted to be published, and that was my dilemma.

I confided in a friend who worked in publishing. She said it was hard to publish a memoir unless it was by someone famous, a film star or a sporting hero for example. 'However, if you're really driven to do it, you need a theme,' she said. I decided the theme was 'turning points' as there were several in my life from which I learned a great deal. I tried to write about one of those turning points, but the critic in my head was relentless. *Who the hell are you to tell people about yourself? This is pure self-indulgence.*

On the surface, my life continued normally throughout my middle fifties. I went to work, enjoyed time with my family and friends, and took an intense interest in politics and the world around me. I cooked, shopped, walked, read, watched movies and listened to music. I led a full life, but underneath I was constantly returning to my problem, like a drinker secretly visiting the liquor cabinet.

My husband, loving and concerned, suggested I get a new job. I kept my part-time job in the corporate world, but in my spare time took on a community project. For a while it seemed like the answer. I threw myself into it with delight, drawing on the skills I'd learned in various jobs, organising, networking, fund-raising and problem-solving. But after a few months the project became onerous and I lost heart. I'd taken a wrong turn. I suddenly realised that the last thing I wanted at this stage of my life was a job with constant stress and frustrations.

My mother became ill and I concentrated on looking after her. Months went by. When she recovered, I thought about writing again. This time I thought I'd write a book that was impersonal, a journalistic kind of book. I searched around for a topic, but my heart was not in it. Something was still pulling me back to the past.

Then I had a breakthrough. I read a book called *Facing the Fifties*, by the writer and Jungian therapist Dr Peter O'Connor. It described the transition from fifty to sixty in a way that explained exactly how I felt. I realised that my stumbling around for the past few years was not crazy, but was in fact quite normal.

During your fifties, O'Connor says, you are in a transitional period. You have to face the loss of children, parents, sexual potency, looks, energy, work and status. You have to face the fear of ageing and face up to your own mortality. You are in a seesaw between *Eros* (Love and Life) and *Thanatos* (Death.) During this period you move from the values of the outer world (status, power, success, action, strength, sexual prowess etc) to the values of the inner world. Sometimes you move from a false self to your true self and throw off those things which no longer have meaning for you.

Often, he says, the false self has been driven by the need to comply with others and to be concerned with 'what others think.' The child (especially the female child) adopts this as an overcoat to protect herself from rejection, but if there has been too much 'giving in' at the expense of the true self, it becomes a barrier to your psychological development. The middle class family is the bastion of the false self, where honesty is buried under niceness and appearances. Males exhibit the false self differently, he says, not by compliance but by belligerence.

When I read this, it explained a great deal. Yes, I had grown up in a family that cared a great deal about appearances. Problems were hidden. My parents were loving and attentive, but they were also perfectionists. My father was very critical, of himself and others. If I got ninety-nine out of a hundred at school, he did not give praise, because that would have given me a swollen head. He simply asked what I got wrong and why. This made me feel that nothing was ever good enough. We children were supposed to be well-dressed, well-behaved and to excel at our schoolwork.

My brother, who was the eldest, rebelled against this pressure and was constantly in trouble. He started truanting from school at a young age, and my father gave him severe beatings. I was afraid of what happened to my brother and tried very hard to be good. I loved my father but I was wary of him. He was calm and gentle most of the time, but had an angry time-bomb inside and could explode without warning.

If I got things wrong I was criticised by my father or teased by my siblings, so I learned to watch what I said. My little sister was treated like a baby and it was my role to help look after her. I was the one in the middle, trying desperately to do things right and to be the helper in the family, the one who could be relied on.

I carried this role into adult life – the helper, the hard worker, the one who kept her problems to herself. It took me a long time to learn that helping others is not always a good thing, because sometimes you end up sacrificing your own needs. But it's hard to throw off the conditioning of childhood, and now in my fifties I could see that I was at it again, being the dutiful daughter and sometimes resenting it.

In O'Connor's book I read that there is a movement to the true self at adolescence (for me it was in my twenties when I left home,) at mid life and again in your fifties. He says the true self does not worry about disapproval. The true self accepts that others may not understand. The true self is the source of creative life. The workaholic is a person running away.

O'Connor says the transition from fifty to sixty is like the heroic journey of great literature. The hero goes away, fights some monsters and returns, bearing wisdom. The first stage (roughly fifty to mid fifties) is a mourning stage. We need to mourn what is lost and face up to it. The process is slow and can lead to depression, apathy, inertia and disillusion. We review our life, our goals, hopes, fears and failures. We look back at the good and the bad memories.

The second stage (roughly mid fifties to fifty-eight) is the doorway to the next age. Our sense of identity is in flux and we have to let go of the ego, which seeks approval. We spend more time in reflection, musing and recollection. We feel helpless at seeing death ahead and sometimes feel finished and passed over. We need to confront these feelings and grieve over them. If they get the upper hand, anger can turn into feelings of depression, envy, regret and guilt. The true self accepts death, which is a humbling experience.

The third stage, he says, is a return to the world, usually from the late fifties to the age of sixty and beyond. We bring back wisdom and truth. We are more tolerant, less judgemental. The payoff is that we expand our horizons. It is a time for new courses, new skills and creative endeavours. The sixties are often a time for meeting our own needs and for serving the community.

He says the journey during the fifties involves doubts and uncertainty. That was certainly my experience. I felt that I was trapped in stage two, unsure how to move on.

In my middle fifties I had also became curious to understand concepts like 'spirituality' and 'the soul.' As an agnostic, I wanted to understand these things without turning to organised religion for explanation. I found some useful ideas in Thomas Moore's book, *Care of the Soul* in which he says the soul needs solitude, contemplation and beauty, such as art and music. He says we need to get away from the daily bombardment of information, and take up something creative such as painting, writing, cooking, sewing or gardening. We need to visit nature, to walk in a park or in the bush. Recording our dreams can help us get in touch with our subconscious. Moore says 'spirituality' and 'religious feeling' can be simply the care of the soul. A sacred object can be your diary, notebooks, paintings or your special letters or photos. These are the concrete forms in which the soul of our lives can be evoked and contained.

I also read wise words from the Dalai Lama. The first level of spirituality, he said, is religion. 'But then there's another level of spirituality,' he added. 'That is what I call *basic spirituality* – basic human qualities of goodness, kindness, compassion, caring. Whether we are believers or non-believers, this kind of spirituality is essential. I personally believe this second level of spirituality to be more important than the first.'

Adeline Yen Mah, author of the best-selling book *Autumn Leaves*, says we ask questions about existence and its meaning when we are young, and we ask those questions again when we feel ourselves growing old. In her fifties she took time out from her busy practice as a doctor in order to write. She said later she had to fight the demons of her childhood by writing it all down. A few years later, she wrote a book about Chinese philosophy. At sixty-two, she said she had never been happier in her life and had reached a place of 'spiritual tranquillity.'

These writers and thinkers helped me to understand my desire to turn my back on the outer world for a while and to write. It was a necessary part of my transition towards sixty.

During this period I had some amazing dreams, which I recorded in my journal. In one, I was stuck in the middle of the road in front of my house, unable to move forwards or backwards, with cars screaming past on either side. I saw that as a metaphor for my life.

In another, I was painting my arms with pink teabags and saying: 'The real me is underneath.' When I woke, I realised that I was putting on camouflage, but that teabags were disposable and I needed to throw them away and find my true self.

In another dream I was pulled into a large old house and wandered from room to room until I found a chapel. When I woke I remembered that in dreams, a house is often a metaphor for your life. In the past, when I dreamed about entering a large old house and wandering through the rooms, it usually meant I was starting a new job or exploring a new area of activity. When I lived in Paris I often dreamed that I was floating above the spires and rooftops of the city, like a figure in a painting by Chagall. Now the dream seemed to be about a search for my inner self, for my spirituality.

In another dream I saw a beautiful cottage by a river. I went inside and sat there feeling peaceful and happy.

I wanted to stay longer, but friends rushed me off and I felt resentful.

Once I dreamt I was with a child on the edge of a snowfield. We came to a house with a lovely garden with every kind of flower. The child wanted to examine them all and I woke up and thought; the child is me, wanting to explore my creative self.

In another dream my husband and I were driving along and saw a sign that said older people must have a more peaceful, balanced life and eat casseroles instead of separate dishes. When I woke up and recorded the dream, I laughed. I reflected that I needed to make this balanced casserole and keep it 'warm.'

My subconscious, through my dreams, was constantly giving me a message.

Now, in a desperate attempt to get past the block in my writing, I had enrolled in a creative writing course in a seaside resort. I finally told my mother when she became stronger and was sent home from the hospital. The doctor thought the fall was a small TIA and warned her that it could happen again. When I said I was going away she looked unhappy, but cheered up when I said that if she became ill again I'd come straight home. We kissed goodbye, and as I left her room I grinned and punched the air with delight at the thought of a week away from responsibilities.

3

Queenscliff

'I looked up in panic and thought, "I can't do this. I'll bet everybody else is writing away like mad."'

I tapped my fingers nervously on the steering wheel as I drove through open farmland to the Bellarine Peninsula. I was looking forward to the week away, but I was anxious. 'What if this is a waste of time,' I thought, 'what if I don't get anything out of it and then I'll be back where I started.' A braver voice chimed in, reassuring me, 'Come on, if you don't like it you can always just pack up and leave.'

'Freefall: Writing without a Parachute' was the name of the week-long writing retreat I was going to at the seaside town of Queenscliff, a couple of hours drive from my home in Melbourne. The teacher was Barbara Turner-Vesselago, a Canadian writer who was visiting Australia. In the back of the car I had my laptop, a printer and a card-table. As instructed, I had also packed food for breakfast and lunches and had made a chicken casserole as my contribution to the evening meal.

I was trying not to get my hopes up. After all, I'd been

on a writing retreat two years earlier, to Varuna in the Blue Mountains. At first I'd been in heaven, with a studio in the former home of the writer Eleanor Dark. I was even given the room she shared with her husband, with a copy of the *Paris Review* 1963 lying on the bedside table as though she had just finished reading the interviews with Evelyn Waugh and S.J. Perelman. I imagined her life there, grounded in the Australian bush while reading about Paris and New York. I pictured her working in her studio or in the garden while her doctor husband was out on his rounds, or sitting by the fire with friends in the evening, talking about writing and politics.

At Varuna I was trying to return to writing after a long gap, but it was hard. At the end of the week all I had was a waste paper basket full of violently screwed up pages and a few sheets of writing about my childhood. Since then I'd struggled with the block in my writing. I tried not to think about that as I pulled up at a guest house by the sea.

The house was light and spacious, with a big kitchen and lounge-room. People were busy finding their rooms and putting food away in the kitchen. Some were setting up their computers in the communal lounge-room. The house had been shut up and we opened the windows and let in the fresh, salty air. When everything was unpacked, we gathered in a circle in the lounge-room. Barbara sat in the centre, a slim woman with curly blonde hair and a wide and welcoming smile. I glanced around the group. There were eleven women and one man, most of them in their fifties like me, but some younger and some older. Barbara opened a folder and said, 'Let's go round the circle. Tell us your first name and why you're here.'

'I'm Sarah,' a tall redhead said hesitantly. 'I've been writing since I was a child. I did a scriptwriting course and worked at that for a few years, but it's a hard world to succeed in. Now I work as a journalist with a women's magazine.'

The man cleared his throat. 'I'm Richard and I'm a radio journalist,' he said and I recognised his voice from the Australian Broadcasting Corporation. He told us that he wrote a variety of things, but mainly science fiction.

Leslie said she was an artist and also loved to write. Gladys was a carer for old people and wanted to record their stories. Cleo was a therapist running a clinic in the Dandenong Ranges and June was a music teacher. When it came to my turn, I felt nervous. There was so much to say, but I wanted to be brief. I told them I'd been a journalist for thirteen years and loved it, and that I'd published a non-fiction book, but then had changed career and worked in a number of different areas. Now my children were grown up and I was working part-time so that I could write, but I was finding it hard.

'I don't want to go back to journalism,' I said, 'I want to write something more creative, more personal, but I'm struggling with a kind of writer's block.' Everybody nodded.

Barbara slipped off her shoes and tucked her feet under her and looked around. 'So many people dream of writing creatively,' she said, 'but their fears get in the way. They never start, or they start and give up. Freefall helps you to get over that. I'm not here to teach you about grammar or technique, although those things may be very helpful later on, but for the moment you're just going to plunge in and write. Most of us write with a critic on the shoulder, telling us that we should write like this and not like that. Sometimes the critic paralyses us. Here you'll learn to write without dividing yourself into the writer and critic. You'll just write. Somewhere further down the line you may look at what you've written and edit it, or it may just turn out to be a part of what gets you to where you end up going, but I don't want you to think about that just yet.'

She outlined the daily schedule. We would write every morning on a topic of our own choosing. At one p.m. we would give her our writing, up to twelve pages double spaced. We were then free to make our lunch and do what we liked until four p.m. For up to three hours before dinner we would meet as a group and she would read some of our work and we would discuss the writing. She would not identify the author of any piece of work, and we were not to ask each other what we'd written. At seven p.m. we'd have dinner together. She asked us not to talk to each other during the morning, so as to give each other space in which to work and think.

We looked at each other nervously and somebody said, 'What are we going to write about?' Barbara outlined four guidelines for Freefall writing. First, write whatever comes up for you. It can be anything at all. 'Don't come with a plan,' she said, 'Just start anywhere and it will lead you somewhere.'

Second, don't change anything as you go along. Put a tea-towel over the computer screen so you can't read it. 'Concentrate on a scene or an event,' she said, 'visualise it and describe it in detail. Don't stop to polish it. Go with the stream of creative thought and see where it leads.

Don't worry whether it's any good or not. The ego, the rational, controlling part of your brain will try to stop you and pull you back to where you feel safe, and these instructions will help you block that out. Normal thinking can take you round in circles, but if you just keep going, the writing will carry you to a different outcome. It will have its own logic.'

The third rule, she said, was to put in all the sensuous detail you could envisage. Move into the scene. What can you see? What can you feel, smell, hear, taste? Be specific. Make sure you are 'showing' and not 'telling.' Telling is summarising – 'on Sundays we used to go for a drive.' But showing is specific and detailed – 'One wet Sunday we got in the old station wagon and Dad said ....'

Fourth, go where you find there's energy flowing. 'You'll feel it within you when you are emotionally connected with the writing,' she said. 'And I don't just mean positive energy. Sometimes the strongest energy is in what we most fear to write about, but follow it anyway. Go "fearward" and don't hold back. What writers seem to fear most is self exposure.'

Ah yes, self exposure. That's what had been holding me back for so long. The inner critic had been dancing around in my head with a witch-doctor's leer, beating a tom-tom. I glanced around the room. The others were listening carefully and taking notes.

'Many people in Freefall choose to write about the past,' Barbara said. 'If you do, you'll find that the material from further back will be more resonant for you than material in the present. Material from the past will be *composted*.'

Before we broke for dinner, somebody said plaintively, 'What if I can't think of anything to write in the morning?' Barbara smiled and said, 'You will. Just start anywhere. If it has no energy for you, try another subject or just press on. Often the energy flags when you're getting close to something you don't want to go near. Go fearwards.'

The next morning we crept about silently like Trappist monks. After breakfast I shut my door, put a tea-towel over my computer and tried to concentrate. Where should I start? Where was the energy? I felt myself being pulled back to the past. I thought of Barbara's words – further back is the best, it's more composted. I put my fingers on the keyboard and typed in a free association fashion about my childhood and about problems with my father. It rambled on for two pages and then stopped. I couldn't go on. I peeked under the tea-towel and read what I had written. I hated it. It was boring and felt like a whinge.

I looked up in panic and thought, 'I can't do this. I'll bet everybody else is writing away like mad.' After a while, I decided to jump forward and write about the good times, about breaking free from my family and going overseas. Yes, that had energy. I would write as though I was talking to Barbara or to a supportive friend. 'If it's not going to be published,' I thought, 'I can write whatever I like.'

I started slowly, thinking my way back to when I was young and setting out to see the world. Soon I was typing more rapidly. From time to time I glanced up – oh that bloody tea-towel – then sank back into the world I was re-creating. After a while I lost all sense of time. I felt almost as though I was in a trance. I felt the energy that Barbara had talked about, or maybe it was just adrenalin. I wanted to have a drink, go to the loo, but I couldn't stop. Around mid-day I paused and looked at my watch. My God, I thought, have I been going that long? It was time to stop, to print it out and give it to Barbara.

I removed the tea-towel and deleted the first few rambling pages, the false start. Then I read what followed:

At the age of twenty-three I left Australia and lived on the other side of the world for three years. London, Paris, Turkey, New York. Sounds like a cigarette commercial. I had wanted to travel since I was twelve. That was the year when I started to learn French and fell in love with the language and poetry of France, borrowed picture books and dreamed of living in a garret and sitting at sidewalk cafes looking out for Simone de Beavoir. Well, that came later, as the dream grew. So I saved up every year through school and university until I had enough to go away for a long time.

I thought I was just on an adventure, to travel and work, to try new things. Looking back I see that it was a crucial turning point, an essential breaking free. All my life I had been the good child, the dutiful one, striving desperately to please my parents with their loving perfectionism. Going to the other side of the world was the only way to be myself, to find out what was important to me, to see them and Australia from a distance.

We sailed away, two girlfriends, blonde and brunette. In those days you went by ship, which was cheap. It took five weeks just to get to Italy and longer to get to

England. You really knew you were going a long way, not like today's twenty-four hour jet planes. Weeks with nothing to do except enjoy yourself. We instantly paired off with two young men. Mine was a tall, dark Yugoslav who was a professional dancer and acrobat. Hers was a Ukrainian Scientologist, travelling to England to study. During the day we swam, sunbaked, walked around the deck and played shuffleboard.

At night we drank rum and coke, ate Greek food in the dining room and danced until we could stand up no longer. Sometimes we kissed in corners or on the deck in the moonlight, standing at the bow of the ship watching the wake behind it. But he was in a dormitory of eight, I was in a bunkroom of four and there was no privacy. It was a lovely shipboard romance without complications, in a time when sex was fraught with problems and lack of contraception.

We shared our table with an English family returning home, a couple and two young children. He had been badly damaged in the war and his face was horribly disfigured. The family was silent and he rarely spoke. Mealtimes were a strain as we tried not to look at him. We made polite conversation which fell into a pool which closed over, no ripples left.

The food was wonderful, new to our palates. Entrees were little mezze, meatballs, dips and spicy vegetables. This was followed by meat and pasta, always plenty. The Aussies on board lined up bottles of tomato sauce, Vegemite and Milo beside their tables and tried to smother away the Greek taste. We thought they were stupid and stuck to our European men as we glanced sideways at the handsome Greek officers in their crisp white uniforms.

When we reached the equator there were ceremonies on board and as the days passed we noticed in the night sky that the stars had changed. It gave us a shock to see that the familiar constellations – the Southern Cross and the Saucepan, were no longer there. It was exciting to be moving so far away. Then one day, as I lay on the *chaise longue* on deck reading and looking at the sea, land appeared – brown and flat and dusty – and someone yelled out that it was Africa.

Africa! It sounded so exotic. I thought of Dr Albert Schweitzer in the jungle and the 'jungle doctor' missionary books I read as a child. I looked across and marvelled that this empty, barren piece of land was really Africa. We had not seen land for weeks, and here it was, proof that we were very, very far from Australia. We were shedding miles, shedding responsibilities, shedding our past selves. We were young and alive and ready for adventure, and it was all happening.

A few weeks later we docked in Naples and said goodbye to our boyfriends. We took a train to Switzerland and on to Germany where we bought a small, second-hand Volkswagen. It gave us freedom and security, like a snail with its house on its back, and we drove all over Europe, from the mountains of Yugoslavia to the back roads of Spain. We ended up in London, where we got jobs and shared a damp, basement flat with two English girls. This was the mid sixties; the time of Swinging London, Carnaby Street and the Beatles.

After six months in London, I set out on another adventure. This time I was truly alone, taking another plunge into the unknown, an even bigger adventure. I took a night plane from London to Paris. My plan was to find a place to live, a job if possible, and to study French at the Sorbonne. On the plane the man next to me introduced himself as Conrad Rooks, a film producer who had just made a film called *Siddhartha*. He had an American accent and showed me a glossy brochure about the film. He was interesting and when he offered me a lift in a taxi, I agreed. I felt happy with my new red raincoat and a brand new life opening up.

I told him the name of the hotel I had booked, and he said he would go to his apartment first and then I could take the taxi on. We drove through small, winding streets and suddenly came to an elegant building with steps up to a large door. The door opened and a beautiful dark young woman flung herself at my companion. Then she saw me in the car and started shouting abuse at him in French. He smiled at me, paid the driver and wished me well. I never saw him again, but it was a great start, the first of many adventures.

I had to come this far away, alone and without support, to find out who I was and what I wanted to be. I wanted to test myself, to survive on my wits and abilities without my family and their expectations. I got a job and my room in a garret. I fell in love, passionately and disastrously, with a married man. The feelings were so deep that his blood seemed to be my blood, and when we finally parted, some years later back in

Australia, I lost the will to live for a while, until common sense slowly returned.

What else happened in Paris? I started to write – a journal, long letters home, and some short stories which I threw in the bin. Most important of all, I discovered myself and what was important to me, and started shakily in the direction my life was to take. I also discovered what I loved about Australia, by distancing myself and forgetting it, apart from brief flashes of memory.

I stared at the computer screen and wondered what Barbara would make of it. She's right about the method, I thought, all this just poured out without stopping. I corrected a few typos and resisted the desire to edit further. It felt embarrassingly personal, but there was no time to change anything, so I printed it out and went to find Barbara. After lunch I went for a long walk on the beach. I had written something, but I didn't know if it was any good. I saw red-headed Sarah in the distance. We waved and kept walking. I was quite glad about the rule of silence. I didn't really want to talk to the others, there was too much to think about.

In the late afternoon we gathered in the lounge room and Barbara asked us how we had felt about the morning's work. Most of us had given her a few pages. One woman said she couldn't think of anything to write and went for a walk instead. 'That's okay,' said Barbara, 'try again tomorrow.'

Barbara told us how she discovered this method called 'Freefall.' She did her PhD at Cambridge University on

Virginia Woolf. She did masses of research, but could not write the thesis. In desperation, she asked an old professor for help. He told her to write fifteen pages a day and bring them to him. By pushing herself to write every day, despite her feeling that most of it was rubbish, she put words on paper. By the fifth day she suddenly saw the whole point of her thesis in a flash. She realised in effect, that Virginia Woolf went into a trance state when she was writing, and went where the trance took her. Suddenly the research fell into place and Barbara completed her thesis quickly.

Later, when she was teaching in West Africa, she discovered that her students were full of stories that just flowed onto the page. They weren't hampered by issues of style or self-criticism. 'I was envious of that,' she says, 'because I was so stuck in academic writing that I couldn't write anything else.' She went to a writing school in Banff where the method was to just pour out whatever you wanted to write, and people read it and told you what worked in what you had written.

'I developed that technique further and have been teaching it all over the world for nearly twenty years,' she said. 'In a group setting like this it works best because the group develops its own energy.' I looked around the group and thought yes, she's right. There was a feeling of being shut off from the rest of the world and going deep into oneself to write. The silence during the day was helping this process.

Barbara then started reading from the morning's writing. One member of the group had written about being placed in an orphanage when she was four. It was chilling and quite moving. Someone else – I presumed it was Richard – had written a science fiction story. Another person had written a beautiful piece of memoir about a small child in a country town on her first day of school. The child started walking to school but was afraid of wolves in the forest and a huge girl called Gloria Gribbles who would bash her up. Eventually she turned around and headed back home. Her father offered her a penny to go to school but she rejected it. Her mother said simply, 'Oh, you're back,' and went on doing the washing. We saw the child's relief and the parents' love. The story was perfect.

Barbara took the lead in discussing each piece after reading it out. We talked about the writing in terms of what worked for us rather than what did not work. There was no place for demolishing another person's confidence, and nor would we have wanted to, for the writing was astonishingly good.

As the pages mounted up, I started to feel worried. She had not read mine. Perhaps she had not had time to read it, or it was not good enough. Then she picked up the last few pages and started to read. It was mine. I felt embarrassed and quite exposed, but then remembered that nobody knew who had written it. They listened intently. When Barbara finished, there was silence. I assumed they hated it and were too polite to say so.

Then Sarah leaned forward. 'I really liked the voice in that piece,' she said, 'I wanted to know more about that person.'

June said, 'I could just picture the red coat. I could see it as a shiny red plastic one.'

'It brought back memories for me,' said another. 'I remember those days of going on a ship and appreciating Australia from far away. I still do that every time I go overseas.'

Barbara nodded and said, 'This piece gives us a glimpse of enticing worlds, which I for one would love to know more about. It's just an overview really and the writer could now slow down a bit and open up those worlds. She does that for a few moments on board ship, but then she rushes forward again. I'd like to know more about the love affair for example.'

'Oooh yes,' said Leslie, the artist. 'It was so powerful when she said "his blood was my blood".'

'You're such a romantic,' said Richard. We all laughed. I felt like hugging them. They liked it! They wanted to hear more! I was astonished.

'You see how this method helps you bypass the inner critic,' Barbara said. 'It's like jumping out of a plane, freefalling into your subconscious mind, which is the source of your creativity. Writing in a group like this helps the process. We all think our writing is terrible, but when you write from the heart, it speaks to others and moves them, and you can see that it has moved them.'

'Will you be talking to us about how to get our work published?' said June.

Barbara shook her head. 'You're putting the cart before the horse. This is about a process, about opening up the writing vein. If you really want to write, you should do it on a regular basis and see what comes up for you. Further down the track you might think about how to edit it, structure it and turn it into short stories, poems or even a book. But that's a long way ahead and not what we're here for. Forget the outcome at this stage and concentrate on the process.'

After the discussion I headed for the kitchen where I was rostered to help prepare dinner. I thought about what Barbara had said. Forget the outcome. That sounded like a good idea, but a scary one, like a journey without a map or destination. I wondered what I would write about the next day. I had no idea, but perhaps something would come up. And first there was dinner, some wine and a chance to get to know the others.

4

Eastern View

'The writing course was restoring my sense of hope about the future. Looking after my mother, however, was making me face up to her mortality and my own.'

The next morning when I sat at the computer, I felt like a cricket ready to jump. I thought about what I had written the day before, about breaking away from home. Barbara had said this piece of writing revealed enticing worlds she wanted to know more about. The group did too; they especially wanted to know more about my love affair. Suddenly I felt afraid. I didn't want to write about that, even though she said we should 'go fearward.' My heart jumped up and down in my chest as I thought about it. Time was slipping away and I was paralysed. Then I made a rapid decision. I would not 'go fearward.' I would write about something completely different, something cheerful.

I cast my mind back to the happiest memories of my childhood. The image that came to mind was Eastern View. I decided to write it as a piece of fiction. I would tell a story based on my parents' visit there when they were courting. I invented a couple called Robert and Silvana, and started writing in the third person.

As they rounded the point at Airey's Inlet and came along the Great Ocean Road, the surf pounding on their left, Silvana became excited. 'It's not much further,' she told Robert. 'Just up the road. They'll all be here, it will be such fun. I'm simply dying to introduce you.' She glanced at Robert, wanting him to share her excitement. His face was serious, watching the road.

I stopped writing. This didn't feel right. There was no energy.

I thought of Barbara's rules. *Imagine a scene and describe it in detail, what you can see, hear, smell etc.* I closed my eyes and went into a daydream about Eastern View and those carefree days. I could feel the sun on my face and hear the sound of the crickets in the garden. I saw my cousin Diana in shorts and bare feet. I decided to switch to the first person and write it as a piece of memoir. I started typing slowly. This time it worked. Now there was plenty of energy. Soon I was plunging down into that dream state again, typing at a slow but steady pace.

When I left Australia and lived on the other side of the world, the only time I felt home-sick was when I thought of Eastern View, the place of my childhood holidays.

Eastern View is a tiny collection of houses on the

Great Ocean Road, south-west of Melbourne. There are no shops, just a small string of houses along the road, masked by trees, with wild bush behind them. The houses are right on the road, facing the sea, a beautiful stretch of wide, white sand and crashing surf.

The houses burned down in the Ash Wednesday bushfires of 1983 and have been rebuilt with modern glass and timber structures, rearing out of the bush on stilts. The place is no longer the same. I prefer to keep my memories intact, of the carefree summers in 'Bills O'Jacks,' the magical house built by my cousins' grandfather. (Not Pa, the lovely pipe-smoking grandpa we shared, but their other grandpa, whom I never met.)

It was an old house, high above the road, reached by a dense garden of native bush interspersed with blue Agapanthus and red hot pokers. A curved stone path followed a gentle rise to the house, but we kids preferred to wrestle our way through the old steps straight up from the road, overgrown by the mysterious, dark garden smelling of eucalyptus and rustling with small lizards.

The lower floor of the house, made of grey stone, was entered by a wooden door in the middle, with two bunk-rooms either side, one for boys and one for girls. My cousins' grandfather had brought the bunks and basins from a ship. The bunks were framed by a metal rail, with a small net basket above your head where you could put your books. Later on, it was where I put my tin of bobby pins so I could curl my hair each night, silently, desperate not to wake my cousin. The room held nothing more than the four bunk-beds and a shipboard basin which pulled out from the wall and had little gold taps.

As soon as we arrived, Diana and I tumbled into the bunk room to choose our beds and giggle. I was tall, skinny and very shy. I was the one who hung back, observing everything. Di was the opposite, a quick-talking tomboy who was fearless. She led me into adventures, told me shocking gossip, made me weak with laughter, and made fun of my fears and insecurities. Each holiday I returned home and told my mother how Di had teased me, but when summer came around I begged to stay with her again because she was such fun.

The top floor of the house was the adult's domain. We went in the back door to the cool, quiet kitchen where my aunt produced delicious cakes, biscuits and roast dinners from an old wood-fire stove. Next to the kitchen was the long, wood-panelled dining room with a table that could seat twenty or more, and a stone fire-place so large you could walk into it. The dining room opened onto a closed-in veranda which faced the sea, and here we spent rainy days, playing 'Five Hundred' or Monopoly, while my aunt read books in her room at the end of the veranda and my older cousins came and went with their friends.

After dinner, we kids did the dishes, taking it in turns to wash and dry. Di taught us to sing 'rounds' like
> *'Kookaburra sits on the old gum tree-ee,*
> *Merry, merry king of the bush is he-ee,*
> *Laugh kookaburra, laugh kookaburra,*
> *Gay your life must be.'*

We sang songs with endless verses, like the one which went

'Oh you can't go to Heaven, (oh you can't go to heaven),
With chewy on your chin, (with chewy on your chin),
Or you'll stick to the gate, (you'll stick to the gate),
As you pass in, (as you pass in)'

And when we ran out of the verses we knew, we made up new ones.

Music and laughter were always present in that house. Di taught my little sister and me to play wooden recorders. We played or sang in harmony for hours, in our bedroom or in the back seat of the car on the long journeys from our house in Melbourne to Eastern View.

On hot days we ran across the road to the beach, clutching old towels and wearing rubber bathing caps with a strap under the chin. Di plunged straight into the surf and thrashed around like a seal. I always hung back, afraid of the cold, until her scorn forced me to plunge in, eyes shut, nose stinging with salt water, lungs bursting. We tried to body-surf, unsuccessfully, but mostly we just dived under the giant waves and bobbed up the other side, caught our breath and then went under again before the next one.

After swimming, we would run along the long, empty beach and back. Then Di would make me lie down on the hard, flat sand with my arms and legs outstretched, and draw around me with a pointy stick. She would write my name underneath, and I would do the same for her. These 'portraits' stayed on the beach while we played, until the tide washed them away.

My cousins' house had a small bathroom with a tin bathtub and a cold water shower which worked when you pulled on a chain. The toilet was a small wooden shed up the hill, a long way from the house. You reached it by a winding path, overgrown with bush, with the smell of toilet and disinfectant getting stronger as you approached. Under the toilet seat was a large hole in the ground, dug by the men in the family. I sat on the wooden seat, my hand over my nose to stifle the pungent smell, and worried about the spiders my cousin told me lurked there and the snakes in the bush outside.

At night-time, we were supposed to use this toilet, and were given a torch with a feeble light to show us the way. If I woke in the night, needing to go, I lay in bed trying to make up my mind whether to brave the snakes and the spiders and the dark, to the toilet up the hill, or whether to incur Di's wrath if I went in the bushes. One night I lay there, listening to the surf crashing in the moonlight, until I could wait no longer. I crept out of bed in my pyjamas and into the bushes just below our window.

My feet crunched on twigs and leaves, a branch scratched my face, and my trickle of water sounded like a waterfall. Suddenly my cousin was at the door, peering out into the darkness in her pyjamas. 'What are you doing?' she hissed, 'Go up to the toilet where you're supposed to go. And don't leave drips on the seat like you usually do.' I was mortified, but it was too late, I'd finished. I crept back into bed and pulled the blankets up high, waiting for sleep.

Mealtimes in my cousins' house were difficult for me because of my shyness. The long table was piled high with food, and my numerous cousins and friends sat on long benches either side. They ate, talked, laughed and fooled around in boisterous activity. I tried to sit at the end of the table and hoped not to be noticed. To be noticed was a terrible thing, because people looked at you and expected you to speak, and usually you were only noticed when someone made fun of you. So I kept my head down and ate and listened, and as soon as the meal was over I busied myself with clearing the dishes.

Dredging up these memories, I suddenly realise that my father suffered in the same way, in the same room, years before I was born. My father used to tell the story of how he nearly did not marry my mother. He was painfully shy as a young man – tall, thin and sensitive. He was attracted to my mother for being all that he was not. She was small, dark and vivacious; always talking and laughing.

When they were engaged, she took him to Eastern View to meet her extended family. My father entered the dining room and fell silent in the face of this noisy mob. He came from an intellectual family who read books at the table and brought up their children to speak only when spoken to. He was intimidated by his parents and forced his way on in the world through brains and ambition, but remained an introvert.

In the face of this noisy, happy family, he felt a failure. He sat there, more and more miserable, convincing himself that he could never fit in, never be like these bright, tennis playing, singing and dancing young men and women. When they spoke to him, he took time to think of a reply and then found that the conversation had rushed on without him.

Later that day he told my mother he wanted to talk to her alone. They went for a walk on the beach and he blurted out his agonised decision – that they should not marry. She was appalled. 'But we've been so happy,' she wailed, 'and the wedding is all arranged! I've made my trousseau and my cousin is lending me her wedding dress. What on earth has come over you?'

My father, sunk in misery, told her he could never fit into her family. He could never make her happy, they were too different. She should marry someone more outgoing like herself. He could not change, it would not work out. My mother pleaded with him and then flew back to the house in floods of tears.

Her mother (my grandmother) was a wise woman. The next day she made up a delicious picnic hamper and told my mother and father to take it and go away alone for the day. They drove along the coast, mostly in silence. They reached a nice, isolated beach and sat under a tree. My mother unpacked the picnic and smiled at my father bravely, offering him food. Something shifted in his heart, and he saw how beautiful she was. The pain in his heart vanished. He took her in his arms and told her he loved her and needed her. The marriage went ahead.

I stopped typing and looked up at the window. The piece seemed to be finished. I removed the tea-towel and read what I'd written. To my amazement, it seemed to have almost written itself. There was a beginning, a middle and an end, which just came out of nowhere. I felt tired and drained as I corrected some typos and printed it out.

At the afternoon session I waited impatiently for Barbara to read my piece. Would they like it? My stomach tightened. When Barbara read it out, there was once again a long silence. Then she said, 'I loved the sense of place this writer has managed to evoke. There's a nostalgic, almost dreamlike quality to it, and when it moves into more specific scenes as it evolves, there's a wholly different kind of immediacy and emotional depth. But even in the more general, dreamlike opening sequence, it's the specific details that bring it alive for me, like the lizards and the gold taps.'

'Yes,' said June, 'and the bobby pins, I remember doing that too.'

Leslie, the artist, joined in. 'I loved the last three lines, especially when she said, "his heart shifted".'

'Still the Romantic,' said one of the others and they laughed.

Sarah said, 'I liked the way the writer stood back, observing, then went into the action and then out again. I also liked the way she got from the childhood story to the father. I don't know how she did that.'

'I liked the way it revealed the house slowly,' said Cleo, 'it didn't describe it all at once, but described a bit of it, then some action, then another bit.'

I listened to the discussion in amazement. I didn't know I was doing all that, I just typed and the story told itself. Barbara's words seemed to be coming true, that if you could get the critic off your back, the writing would find its own logic. I tried to wipe the smile off my face, since I was not supposed to reveal who had written it.

Barbara read some more pieces from the morning's writing. Someone had written a piece about boarding school. The detail was so good I could imagine myself as one of the girls hunched over the scrubbed table in the kitchen at night, drinking cocoa, whispering about the horrible headmistress who was making their lives miserable.

'As a general rule,' Barbara said, 'try not to make your villains completely black. If you do, it will be hard for the reader to believe in them. Try to give them some redeeming characteristic, no matter how small. Perhaps the headmistress loved her small dog, for example.'

I thought about *Anna Karenina*, which I had just read again after a long gap. When I read it at university, I thought Anna was right to leave her husband, Karenin, because he was boring and his ears stuck out. Reading it forty years later I saw that Karenin was not actually so bad. He was a cold civil servant who did not understand his wife, but when he found out she had a lover, he offered to turn a blind eye as long as she would not publicly disgrace him or have her lover in the house. Anna, who was sometimes quite silly, refused this olive branch and flaunted her lover in public, even though it meant putting herself outside the pale of her society. Leaving her husband also meant abandoning her child. That did not bother me at eighteen, but it bothered me a lot when I read the book forty years later. I thought how clever Tolstoy was, constantly shifting our opinion of the main characters.

Yes, Barbara was right; characters should not be all good or all bad.

I came out of my reverie to hear Barbara reading a piece about a young man going to war. I assumed it was written by Richard. I liked his quiet presence and the fact that he did not mind being the only man amongst this group of women. Someone else had written about climbing a rock face, with great suspense.

The next piece was about a woman whose son was schizophrenic and a drug addict. We hung on the words as the son veered unpredictably from infantile behaviour to violence. The mother acted with love and patience, but we sensed her growing desperation. I glanced around the room and wondered who had written it. Everybody seemed to be producing remarkable writing, vivid and often very personal. Barbara pointed out that some of these pieces were examples of 'going fearward.'

'The greatest barrier to writing is the internal critic,' she said. 'Make a list of what it says when it criticises your writing.'

We started scribbling furiously. I wrote, 'Self indulgent, too exposing, too serious, too heavy, lifeless.'

'Now,' said Barbara, 'underline the most important one.'

I underlined 'self indulgent.'

Barbara asked what we had written and we went round the circle. The lists were fairly similar, which was comforting.

Barbara smiled. 'The internal critic is very powerful, especially when you write personal material. Take the word you have selected as your worst fault and write for a few minutes without stopping, about what your writing would be like if you were to give that quality full rein.'

I found a clean page in my note book and wrote:

If I were to be totally self-indulgent I would write about the taboos and secret parts of my life, the joys and pain, without censorship. I would not worry about hurting others, shocking others or appearing vain or a victim. I would write to liberate my stories, to record and examine them, to make sense of my life. To see where I have come from and where I should go next. To float free of the suffocating cloak of respectability I have always worn. To cry out: 'This is me,' when I was brought up to do the opposite.

Barbara asked if anyone wanted to read out what they had written. Sara said she feared that her writing was 'trivial' and read out some deliberately trivial writing about tram timetables, which turned out to be quite funny. As we started laughing she looked surprised, and then started laughing herself.

June thought she had 'poor me' writing and read out a paragraph on this. She wrote that she was sure everyone hated her writing and in the end even her dog seemed to turn up his nose at it and left the room when she read her writing out loud. We laughed and laughed and felt our fears diminish. We felt drawn together by the common fear that our writing was no good.

'Now you see what can happen if you throw off your internal critic,' Barbara said. 'Don't let it cut off your creative voice.' I looked at what I had written and wondered if I could be brave enough to write without fear of self-exposure or self-indulgence.

At the mealtime that night everyone was relaxed and talkative. Most people said the course was rewarding. Some of them were just doing it as a hobby, taking a break from their regular job. For me, it was more important than that. It was throwing up difficult questions. I was phasing out my current job and trying to work out what the next stage of my life would be. Should I look for a new job or should I 'retire' and write full time?

After dinner I went to my room and phoned Race. I told him how well things were going and that they liked my writing. 'That's wonderful, darling,' he said, 'Show me what you've written as soon as you come home.' I smiled. It was good to hear his strong voice and to know that he was happy for me. We talked about what he'd been doing and news of family and friends. 'By the way,' he said, 'your mother wants you to call her.'

'Is she all right?' I started to feel anxious.

'Yes, I think so. She just wants to hear your voice.'

I dialled her number and thought, *please don't get sick again.* She had come out of hospital two weeks earlier and had made a good recovery, but I knew the retirement home would phone me if she was really ill.

'Oh thank goodness you've called,' she said in a weak voice. 'When are you coming back?'

'At the end of the week. Are you okay?'

'Not really.' The TV was blaring in the background and I asked her to turn it down. There was a long pause while she rustled the newspaper, dropped the remote control, muttered, found it and turned off the TV.

I shut my eyes and saw it all. She was in her usual place

at this time of night, in bed in her cosy room in the retirement home. Her room looked onto a courtyard garden and was filled with her favourite things – my father's roll-top desk, a painting of northern Victoria where she grew up and a painting of the beach at Beaumaris, not far, she always told us, from the place where my father proposed to her one moonlit night. Under the window were two pale blue armchairs where she entertained her friends with a cup of tea or a brandy and dry.

'I'm a bit off colour,' she said. 'I felt rather dizzy this morning so I spent the day in bed. I got them to phone the doctor. He thinks it's my blood pressure and told me to rest for a day or two.'

'That's good advice, don't get out of bed.' I knew that she was well looked after and that her friends in the retirement home would be dropping in to see her. We talked for a while about her health and I said I would visit her as soon as I returned home.

'All right, I don't want to be a bother to you. Good night darling.'

'Sleep well. I love you Mum.'

'I love you too.' She blew kisses down the phone.

I hung up and wrapped the doona around me for comfort. I felt a little depressed after talking to my mother. The happy mood I had been enjoying during the afternoon had disappeared. I reflected that she had not asked a single question about how I was, or what I was doing. Perhaps I couldn't expect that any more. In the past she'd always been strong and cheerful, but now she'd become panicky and needy.

'She's afraid of what lies ahead,' I thought, 'I might be

the same when I get to her age, or well before that.' I thought again about the fifties being a seesaw between Life and facing up to one's inevitable decline.

The writing course was restoring my sense of hope about the future. Looking after my mother however, was making me face up to her mortality and my own. In two years I would be sixty. I didn't feel old, but it sounded old. Already I was finding it hard to hear in noisy restaurants or when people spoke softly. My eyes were deteriorating too. 'Only twenty years more and I'll be eighty,' I thought. 'By then I might be deaf or blind or have Alzheimer's!' I felt a shiver of fear. Time was running out. Sometimes I felt calm about that. After all, I'd had a rich and varied life so far, and done most of the things I wanted. But at other times I felt like Dylan Thomas, *'Do not go gentle into that good night/Rage, rage against the dying of the light.'*

A nightmare woke me in the early hours of the morning. It was about my mother. We were in a Mini-Minor, driving on a road which ran in a straight line across a weir. The water on either side of us was calm, but then the waves got bigger. As I drove I thought, 'You could drown if you were out there.' Suddenly the waves were huge. I reached a wire fence on the side of the weir. The waves were now enormous. There was no way out and we were going to die. I thought, 'If I had a rope I could secure the car to the fence,' but I didn't have a rope. I woke up in a sweat, my heart pounding. I stared into the darkness and thought, 'I can't save her from death or myself either.'

5

Greek policemen

'This is the way to write, I thought, without worrying about what it's for or whether it will be published.'

The next morning I felt like writing something different. I flipped through the filing cards of memory and ended up in Greece, decades earlier. A story immediately sprang to mind, one with drama and suspense. It had happened over thirty years ago but was still vivid in my mind. I closed my eyes and called up the scene for a while, then started typing.

We left Athens early and drove north, heading for Yugoslavia. In the youth hostel we met two Austrian boys who asked if they could have a lift. They seemed harmless, so we agreed, thinking that they might be protection against the Greek men. They spoke little English, so we didn't talk much, and when we did it was a garbled mixture of English, German, French and pantomime. I liked their open-ness and simplicity. I first met them when I was passing the door to their bunkroom on the way to the bathroom at the hostel.

They were sitting on the lower bunk eating bread and sausage. I said hello, and Helmut said *Guten Morgen,* while Andreas said 'We are making ze pic-nic.'

They were happy to sit in the back of the car, while Zoe and I took turns to drive. The little Volkswagen was as reliable as ever, never letting us down even on dusty, pot-holed roads or on steep mountain passes. By mid-afternoon we started looking for the youth hostel at Mount Olympus. On the map, it appeared to be in a monastery, or near a monastery, it was not clear. We were climbing higher, mist swirling around the mountain as the road curved through dense pine forests. Then one of the boys shouted out, and we saw the battered sign with the word *Monasteria.*

We turned onto the narrow track and then up a driveway leading to an old, stone building. We parked the car and walked to the door and knocked. Silence. We knocked again. Eventually a tall man came to the door, dressed in the black gown of a Greek Orthodox monk, with long grey hair and beard. We asked about the youth hostel, but he just stared at us. Helmut stepped forward and mimed sleeping, his head sideways on his hands, and then eating. The monk considered this and then gestured for us to follow him.

He led the way into a small room facing the driveway. It was dark, with a wooden floor. There was only one piece of furniture in it, a small wooden table. The monk went away, and came back with a jug of water, a loaf of bread that looked like a stone and a small bowl of black olives. He spread out his hands, to indicate that this was ours for the night.

'Youth hostel?' said Zoe, 'hostel?' The monk looked puzzled, shook his head and pointed down the road. He started backing out of the room. I said *Toilet? Toiletten?* Wondering what the Greek word was. He pointed out the window, down the driveway, and disappeared.

We looked at each other and Zoe said, 'This is not a youth hostel.' Andreas and Helmut muttered together in German and Helmut said, 'We stay. Is free.'

I said to Zoe, 'I have to go to the loo, will you come?' We left the boys and walked down the driveway, and soon found it by the smell. I pushed open the wooden door, releasing a swarm of buzzing flies, and looked in. It was a small concrete room with a dirt floor and a hole in the middle, spilling over with raw sewage. A large wooden stick rested upright by the hole, presumably for poking down your latest offering. The smell was almost unbearable, but I held my breath and squatted over the hole and then rushed outside. Zoe then took her turn and reeled out, swatting away the flies. 'Bloody, hell, I'm not staying here,' she said. 'Let's go back to the nearest town and look for the youth hostel.'

We grabbed the boys and drove down the mountain, soon finding a turn-off to a small Greek village. We drove slowly up and down the streets until we found the familiar youth hostel sign. It was a simple wooden building, facing the main street. We tried the door. It was open. There were only two rooms, with bare boards and metal bunks.

'We're sleeping here,' I said to the boys. 'Let's go and look for something to eat.' We drove slowly through the town, looking for a café. Suddenly a fat man walked up to the car, dressed in a dark green uniform, and signalled us to pull over. He came round to the driver's window and peered in, looking at each of us in turn. He breathed garlic over us while he looked in, and then ordered us to come into the building next to the car. He led us into a simple concrete room and sat down at a large desk, yelling out towards another room. He gestured for us to sit on the rough benches around the walls, and sat back, picking his teeth with the long nail of his little finger.

We asked what was wrong. He pointed to himself and said '*Polizei*' but we could get little more out of him. A thin, worried-looking man scurried in and was given an order. He disappeared. We whispered among ourselves. It seemed that the fat man was the chief of police, and the thin one his side-kick. Other than that we had no idea what was going on. We waited.

Soon the thin one returned with a tray filled with small cups of strong Turkish coffee and glasses of water. These were offered to us. We sipped our coffee. The fat one slurped his coffee, wiped his face with the back of his hand, and muttered to the thin one. Then he looked at us and said loudly '*Passportes!*' We looked at him. He said it again, holding out his hand, becoming red in the face. Zoe and I produced our passports. The boys went back to the car and got theirs from their rucksacks.

The chief of police studied them carefully, fat fingers slowly turning the pages. From time to time he looked up at each of us, then back to the passports. Eventually he pointed to the boys, then to us. 'Married?' he asked. The boys said 'No, no.' I glared at them, not liking the way the policeman had been looking at us. I moved closer to Zoe. 'What do they want?' she muttered.

The fat one then conferred with the thin one in Greek. The conversation went on and on, with glances towards us. The fat one rubbed his chin, and leaned back in his chair. He was perspiring, his shirt strained over his belly and there were dark sweat stains under his arms. The other one looked nervous, unable to meet our eyes. Eventually the chief of police stood up. He gave back our passports solemnly. Then he put on his cap and said: 'Fiesta,' pointing down the road. He waved us out the door, adding 'We go – your car.'

When we got outside, he made the four of us get in the back, while he and his companion went in the front. Zoe and I perched on the boys' knees, heads bent against the roof, barely able to fit in the tiny car. The boys muttered as we wriggled around, trying to get comfortable. It was starting to get dark. The police chief started the car, stalled and started it again. He looked at the gears, fumbled for the lights, put the car in first gear and stalled again. 'He's got the hand brake on,' Zoe whispered in my ear.

Finally he took the brake off and moved the car forward, in fits and jerks, until he was in third gear, driving out of the town and down a dirt track, the car lurching up and down the potholes, the fat policeman hunched over the wheel, looking ahead. Every time the car hit a rock or a hole, Zoe and I bounced up and down, hitting our heads on the roof of the car. The boys were silent, or whispered in German. They seemed quite relaxed, while Zoe and I were tense and worried.

After about forty minutes the lights of a village appeared, and we bumped our way towards it across a field, and jerked to a halt under a tree. We could hear loud Greek music, amplified. The two policemen got out and conferred. We unravelled ourselves and I hissed at the boys, 'Don't leave us alone! Just stick by us!' The chief of police led us towards the village. It was a fiesta, of sorts. People were milling about in a couple of simple cafes, or sitting at tables and chairs outside. On the grass nearby, a lamb was being roasted on a spit, smelling of hot fat and garlic.

The police chief sat us at a table in front of the cafe and ordered retsina. We drank a little and looked around. The band had a singer who was very fat and wailed like a snake charmer while banging a tambourine on her knees, elbows and bottom. Some people looked at us curiously, and nodded in welcome. The chief of police held court, showing off to the crowd. We could not understand what he was saying, but it was clear he was talking about us, mainly to the other men, with much laughter. From time to time he strutted around the other tables, talking to the men and gulping retsina. The thin one looked at him nervously, and then at us.

The boys got up and wandered away to explore the village. Zoe and I started to go after them, but the policeman was by our side, holding our arms, and indicated that we should accompany him while he did his official duties. He filled our glasses. We sipped our drinks and ate lamb and bread. We started to relax. The music got louder, people shouted and laughed, bottles were passed from table to table.

The boys returned and we chatted amongst ourselves. 'He just wanted the car,' they said. 'No need to worry.' We discussed again where we would sleep. 'Please stay with us in the youth hostel,' Zoe begged the boys. But they were adamant; they would stay in the monastery.

Some time well after midnight, the party started winding down. We were tired, but could not leave. Eventually the chief of police finished his conversation with the other men and stood up to go. Again he pushed us into the back of the car, and we lurched slowly back the way we had come. When we reached the village we all got out. We said goodbye to the policemen and drove away quickly.

As we drove up the mountain we all spoke at once, laughing with relief. We dropped the boys at the monastery, promising to pick them up early the next morning. Then Zoe and I drove back to the village, now silent and sleeping. We pulled up at the youth hostel, dragged out our rucksacks and sleeping bags and turned towards the door. Out of the shadows stepped the two policemen. We screamed and ran for the door, making it just before them. We slammed the door behind us.

'Quick, the bunk,' said Zoe, pulling at its metal frame. We heaved and pushed until it was against the door. Then we sat on another bunk, side by side in the dark, waiting for them to break in, too afraid to speak. We could hear them outside the door, speaking in low voices. We waited. After a very long time we heard them walk away. 'We'd better not go to sleep,' I whispered, 'they might come back.' We sat there waiting, but our eyes started to close. We took it in turns to doze and wake.

A few hours later, dawn started filtering through the windows. We dragged the bunk away from the door, threw our things in the car and sped up the mountain. We woke the boys and berated them for leaving us alone. They seemed unconcerned by what had happened. We drove down the mountain. We had to go through the village again to get back on the main road. The streets were deserted. But just before the town petered out there was a small café, and there, sitting at a table drinking coffee, was the chief of police and his sidekick. 'Oh, no,' I shrieked and stepped on the accelerator, speeding away as fast as we could.

That night we ditched the boys and continued north without them.

I smiled as I finished typing the last words. I had enjoyed writing this piece and was amazed at how much I remembered or could invent. This is the way to write, I thought, without worrying about what it's for or whether it will be published. Just writing for the pleasure of it and the ability to recapture a piece from the past and re-live it again.

When Barbara read my story in the afternoon I watched the others and saw that they were hanging on every word. When she read the last line people burst out laughing.

'Oh, I liked that story very much,' said Cleo. 'It was full of suspense, and it was good the way the tension eased off in the middle and then built up again.'

'I really liked the voice here,' said Barbara, 'but for me it was not so much the suspense that stood out, as the I-character's sense of confusion and disorientation – the series of experiences of not knowing. It's like some of the stories of childhood that are being written at this workshop, about the orphanage and the boarding school. Again, those are worlds where you don't know the rules; you don't know what will happen next. The chief of police takes the passports, but will he give them back? It's heightened by the lack of language and being in another culture. It's all a mystery.'

'Those things happen when you travel,' said Leslie. 'They were lucky it didn't turn out worse.'

Sarah burst in. 'I felt so angry with those two boys, why were they so hopeless?'

'They were just along for the ride,' said Richard.

Gladys said quietly, 'I've never been to Greece; I would have liked more description of the country, to set the scene.'

'But she got the five senses right,' said Sarah, 'that toilet, I could smell it, how terrible.'

I listened with delight and tried not to grin like a lunatic. How glad I was to have come to this workshop. It was freeing me from my writer's block.

'I'm giving you back your writing now,' Barbara said. 'You'll see that I have marked a paragraph for each of you, which I want you to open up.'

I looked at my story and saw that she had marked a

section in the first paragraph. It was the part where I had referred to meeting the Austrian boys, saying that I liked their open-ness and simplicity. She had written: '*Show this through a conversation.*'

Barbara looked around the group and said, 'Now get closer to it. Zoom in. Show what you're telling. Don't think about it too much, just write.'

I wondered how to do that, since I couldn't remember anything about the Austrian boys apart from what I'd written. I looked around the group. Everybody was writing, so I picked up my pen and invented a conversation, with a new line for each speaker.

In the youth hostel, we met two Austrian boys who were Art students. When I passed the door to their room on the way to the bathroom, they were sitting on the lower bunk, studying a map and eating some bread and sausage. I said hello, and the thin one with glasses said 'Hi,' with a big smile. The shorter one looked up.

I sat down on the bed opposite and said slowly, 'My name is Helen,' pointing at myself.

The tall one said, 'Helmut,' and then, 'Andreas,' pointing at his friend. He looked at me and said, 'Englisch?'

'Australian.'

They laughed and said, almost together, 'Kangooroo!' There was a silence while we all tried to think of something more to say. Andreas gestured at the food: 'We are making ze pic-nic.'

I nodded and pointed to the map. 'Where are you going?'

They looked at each other. Helmut said, 'Maybe north, maybe south,' and threw up his hands. We all laughed at the deliciousness of being so free, of not knowing where you would be tomorrow.

'And you?' asked Helmut.

'We are going north,' I said, pretending to drive a car. 'To Yugoslavia.'

'Ach, very good. Tomorrow?'

'Yes, tomorrow.'

They looked at each other and spoke quickly in German. Then Helmut said carefully, 'Miss Kangaroo, would you be so kind as to let us go, um, drive in your car?' He had a way of rolling his r's and pausing as he tried to think of the correct English.

They looked at me hopefully, like two puppies. I weighed up their request. They were polite and seemed harmless. Perhaps they would be useful in protecting us from the Greek men. I said slowly, 'I will talk to my friend,' and got up to go.

Helmut rushed to stand up, bumped his head on the bunk, disentangled himself and held out his hand.

'Very nice to meet you,' he said formally. His friend rushed to copy him.

'See you later,' I said, and left them smiling hopefully at me.

I looked up as Barbara said, 'You can stop now. This is an exercise you can practise at home. Open things out. Imagine the scene, get as close up as you can, give us the specific details.'

I looked at what I had written. It felt clunky and

amateurish, but it was another milestone. I had invented all of it, so I was learning to write fiction and dialogue. My father had always told me I should stick to writing non-fiction and that I was not a creative writer. I had believed him. Now I realised that I was only held back by my own fears. The line between fact and fiction was not as impregnable as I had thought. This made me very happy.

I looked up as I heard Barbara say, 'When you get home, make sure you have a regular time for writing if you want to take it seriously. Do it in the same place, at the same time, and stick to your routine.'

A plan formed rapidly in my mind. On the days that I was free, I would write every morning from nine a.m. to one p.m. That would leave the afternoons free to see my friends, family or my mother. I would not worry yet whether it would be publishable. I would just write what 'came up' and see where it took me.

6

Writing and the Demon

'You must be stark, raving mad to write about that affair
you had in Paris. A married man, how shameful, fancy
telling the whole world about it!'

At home the wisteria was in bloom on the front steps
and the gleditsias were covered with tiny leaves like
golden confetti. Spring had arrived. A few days later I was
at my desk in the second bedroom by nine a.m. I'd already
been for my morning walk and read the newspaper, so it
was a good start. I opened my laptop and thought about
what to write.

I was drawn back to Paris, the place where I was first
truly alone, testing my wings, feeling good in my new red
raincoat. Barbara and the group at Queenscliff had liked
this and wanted to know more. It was time to be brave
and 'go fearward.'

I shut my eyes and drifted backwards in time to that
first morning in Paris. It was February 1967, a cold
winter's day. I saw a young woman of twenty-four, slim,
with long blonde hair, standing at the window of a cheap
hotel room on the Left Bank. She looked down on a

narrow, cobbled street. A plump housewife came out of a *boulangerie-patisserie*, carrying an armful of baguettes. A student chugged past on a motorised bicycle, a scarf around his neck. The young woman at the window watched for a while and then suddenly grinned and hugged herself. She was all alone, with very little money. She had to find a job and a place to live, but she was elated. She was looking for love, life and adventure and was sure she would find it.

I started typing. I wrote the scene in the first person, as a memoir. I was amazed at how vividly the memories came back, like scenes from a film, despite the gap of more than thirty years. I remembered Barbara's comment that memories from way back are composted.

I wrote about criss-crossing Paris by foot and on the metro, discovering the city and searching for a job. I then moved forward a few days, to a scene in the breakfast room of the small hotel. I remembered meeting a young American student there, who told me to be careful. He said a girl had recently been murdered in a hotel nearby. She'd gone out with a North African she met in a café and been found dead in her room.

I described this conversation, and my shock at his words. I described the young American and the smell of coffee and croissants, and my decision that it was time to move on. I described how I found a room in the apartment of a rich old lady who was lonely and wanted me to teach her English. I acquired a boyfriend named Georges, an engineer. When he came to visit, the old lady made us play cards and she flirted with Georges. Later on, she read my diary in which I had written about this, and kicked me out. I went to stay in George's apartment, but we fought and broke up.

I looked up from the computer. The story was going too fast, like a runaway train. It was time to slow it down. Perhaps I should go back to how I got my job. Yes, I would describe how finally, when my money had nearly run out, I saw an ad in the *International Herald-Tribune* for a secretary at a small international university, and phoned at once.

As I started to write about the job interview, I suddenly realised that I would need a name, and so would everybody else in the story, even if it was just an exercise in creative writing and would not be published. I was writing a memoir, but it felt as though the girl I was writing about was in some way separate to me. I did not want to use real names, so I called myself Anna Linley.

I described the interview with the office manager, who wanted to give me the job, and then my interview with the president of the university, whom I called Dr Philippe Schumann. Now I had to describe him. I closed my eyes and pictured him at that first meeting – a man of medium height with greying hair and arresting blue eyes. I changed this to 'wavy dark hair' and 'penetrating brown eyes.' I described the brief interview in which he was fast-talking and demanding. He said I was just a tourist who would leave Paris after a short while, but I told him I intended to stay for at least a year. I did a typing test and pretended I had shorthand and hoped they wouldn't find out that I didn't.

As I wrote, I was amazed at how seamlessly the memories were turning into realistic scenes. What had really happened was too long ago to remember in detail, but it was easy to fill in the gaps with my imagination. By opening everything out, I could see the places as clearly as though I'd just left them.

I ended the interview scene with the young woman walking away from the university, delighted that she'd got the job but worried about the president, whom she found abrupt and unfriendly. I read over what I'd written. With some polishing, it would make a first chapter. I liked the way it ended, with the reader wondering how the young woman would fare with this brusque, unappealing man.

I smiled to myself. Yes, the first impression was bad, but it didn't last long. Philippe could be tense and impatient at times, but mostly he was friendly, dynamic and funny. He was the most interesting man I had ever met, full of ideas and energy. I became his secretary and we worked well together. He taught me a lot and gave me more and more responsibility and I loved it.

I met his wife, who worked in the same building, and noticed the coolness between them and wondered what it was about. In June, when the university closed for the summer vacation, I got a job with Club Med and went to Turkey for three months. In September I returned to the university. I realised that I was falling in love with Schumann and resisted. But when two people are working together all day and are attracted to each other, reason often deserts them. Sometime later that year Schumann and I became lovers.

As I thought about this I froze. How could I write this memoir when it would mean revisiting all the joy and pain that followed? I would have to relive my guilt towards his wife, even though they had a very French arrangement whereby both could have discreet affairs. Their agreement had been to stay together for the sake of the children and financial security. I would have to show the conflict that had been in my heart as to whether to stay or go, and why the following year I left Paris and went to New York to work.

I remembered how Philippe had followed me to New York and our joy at being re-united. Then six months later, I returned to Australia and became a journalist. We wrote feverish love letters to each other. I remembered how he came to Australia to talk about marriage and met my parents, who tried to drive him away. Then there was the *dénouement*, the crises in his personal and professional life, the months of waiting, my anger and my final break with him, five years after we had first met.

I thought about the period in which the story was set, of the political events which absorbed us – the Vietnam War, which we discussed almost daily, the civil rights movement, the assassination of Martin Luther King and the assassination of Robert Kennedy. It was a time of student unrest around the world, and then in May 1968, there was the eruption in the streets of Paris and the 'revolution' that nearly toppled the government of General de Gaulle. We were caught up in all that. I was by then living in the heart of the demonstrations, in a small apartment above the Café de Flore on the Boulevard St Germain. The student protests spread to the university where we worked and soon Philippe was struggling to keep control, with his job in danger.

I suddenly felt excited about re-creating those turbulent political times. They would make a dramatic background to the story. But as my thoughts went back to the love story that I had suppressed for so long, I realised that it would be much easier to write about the political events than to write about the love affair and the grief that surrounded it.

Suddenly I felt all the energy leave me. Why did I want to re-visit this story that had been buried for decades in my heart and in a box of old letters? I'd been married to another man for nearly thirty years whom I loved and admired. I was a mother, a step-mother, a step-grandmother and would soon be holding a new grandchild.

Now that all the children had grown up and left home, Race and I were enjoying a peaceful time together, almost a honeymoon. So why was all this coming up? Was it because I now had time to reflect? Was it because Paris was a time of intense feelings, when my heart was completely open and my world was still full of endless possibilities? Was I writing this story in order to heal the wound? I had no answers. I felt daunted by the idea of writing it all down with its myriad twists and turns. I sighed and closed the computer. It was time to give up for the day.

That night, when Race and I were curled up in bed reading, I could not concentrate on my book. My mind was full of what I'd written in the morning and what I would write next. I wondered if it was disloyal to Race to be so involved with a past love affair. I touched his arm and said, 'You know I'm writing all this freefall stuff about my time in Paris, don't you?'

'Mmmm?' He dragged his eyes away from his book and gave me his attention.

'It seems to be pulling me back into that love affair I had before we met.'

'Well that's all right isn't it?'

'If I keep going and it turns into a book, would you think that was disloyal to you?'

He laughed. 'Of course not. Don't be silly. It all happened decades ago.'

'I know, but some men might be threatened.'

'Well I'm not. Silly rabbit.' He kissed the tip of my nose and went back to his book.

I smiled at the way he made light of my fears, like a magician clapping his hands. I lay back and thought about when we first met. It was 1971, about the time I was breaking off with 'Philippe.' Race's wife Jill had died tragically a year earlier, from cancer. She was only thirty-four and had left him with three young children aged eight, ten and twelve.

He had phoned me to discuss an article I'd written in *The Age*. He was then working for Gough Whitlam, who was Leader of the Opposition in the federal parliament. Race was also standing for a seat in the federal parliament. I remembered him at our first meeting, tall, thin and earnest, with dark wavy hair starting to go grey. Now his hair was white.

I thought about our first dinner, when we talked about politics and social issues. It was an exciting time, when it was starting to look as though the Labor Party might win the next election and Whitlam would become Prime Minister. We had plenty to talk about, but it was only a year later that I started to know him intimately, when he told me about Jill and his grief at her death. We'd both lost the person we loved, and it was one of the things that drew us together.

We married in 1972 and at the end of that year Whitlam won the election and Race became a federal MP. I sailed into marriage convinced that I could handle anything, even three stepchildren. I had no idea how hard it would be to make a 'blended' family or how traumatised the children were by their mother's death.

I looked at Race reading his book, deep in concentration, and wondered if he sometimes revisited the past as well. I said, 'Do you think about Jill much these days?'

He put down his book and was silent for a long time. Then he said, 'Yes I do, especially when I see the children and grandchildren. I think it's so unfair, so *bloody* unfair, that she can't see how they've grown up and what marvellous people they are.' I saw tears come into his eyes as he said, 'She's missed all that, you see.'

I put my arms around him and felt tears come into my own eyes. Her death had scarred them all, and when I married him at the age of twenty-nine and went to live in his house – her house – I felt her ghost everywhere. I found her recipes in the kitchen and some of her clothes in a cupboard. When I brought a new wastepaper basket one of the children told me not to move the old one because 'it was Mummy's.'

I wanted to take her place, to make them all happy again. Vanessa, the youngest, accepted me as a stepmother, but Sean and Jane, the older two, found it hard. Their mother was always there between us. They didn't want a replacement, they wanted her. They needed their father, but he was busy in Canberra as a new MP. They saw his love for me and resented it.

We were all miserable in those early years. I had two

babies in quick succession and became exhausted to the point of collapse. My stepchildren struggled through the teenage years, feeling abandoned. I felt resentful to Race for being absent so often. It was only years later and with therapy, that each of us came to understand what had happened to us all. Therapy helped me to save our marriage and keep the family together. Later on I became closer to my stepchildren and they accepted me as a friend, but never as a mother replacement.

Three decades on, the presence of Race's first wife was still with us. Only a few nights earlier, I had seen him with tears in his eyes when we were listening to Beethoven's Ninth, and when I asked why, he said it was the first record he and Jill had bought together. There had been other such moments over the years, but I did not feel jealous because I felt secure in his love for me.

I held him tighter and said, 'we were lucky to find each other all those years ago, weren't we, and to have survived this long together.'

'Absolutely.' He kissed me and said, 'What's the matter?'

'I don't know really. I'm dredging up past memories with my writing. Sometimes it pours out and sometimes I get paralysed by it.'

'If it's important to you, then you must keep going.'

I sighed. 'It's a crazy life though, writing a book that may never be published. You're alone all day with your thoughts and you don't even get out and talk to people.'

'Well, we'll just have to compensate by having people over more often. I'll do the cooking if that will help.' I hugged him and thought how generous he was and how mature. He had encouraged me in everything I had done so far and always would.

That night I dreamed I was a young woman again. I climbed the stairs to my little garret above the Cafe de Flore and met a man who said he was writing a book about Paris. He came closer and I was afraid and ran onto the roof. It was full of people standing around, but they were grotesque, like actors in a Fellini film, with brightly coloured hair and clothes. I didn't want to join this weird crowd. I woke up and thought about the dream. It seemed to mean that going back to Paris was dangerous territory.

A few days later I started the next chapter. I described how I found the room above the famous cafe where Sartre and de Beauvoir had met their friends and written their books. I wrote about working with Philippe every day and becoming attracted to him. The pages mounted up. I sat back and thought about the first time we made love. I remembered a weekend driving around Switzerland, dinners by candlelight and warm beds covered with soft white doonas. I recalled the nervousness I felt on the train going from Paris to Basel to meet him, the mixture of desire and apprehension, of stepping in a dream-like state into the unknown.

I stared at the keyboard and wondered how I could write about our first night together and whether I could ever publish any of this. I started typing but I couldn't find the words. Fear held me back. Soon I felt desperately tired. I wanted to sleep, to escape. I fell onto the bed and closed my eyes. When I woke an hour later, I felt a little better. I lay there and thought about the inner critic that was trying to sabotage my writing.

I pictured it as a demon, peering around the bedroom door. It was like Lucifer, a goat-man with horns and cloven feet and a long tail. It started speaking to me.

Demon: This writing's not very good you know, despite the nice things Barbara said at Queenscliff. She probably says everyone's writing is good, so you have no real yardstick to measure it by.

Me: I think Barbara's honest – if she says something works well for her, it does.

Demon: Well, so what? It won't be good enough to get published, so you're wasting your time.

Me: How do you know it won't be published? I've hardly written anything yet. It might and it might not.

Demon: Well, even if it's published, it'll be torn to shreds by the critics.

Me: Why do I have to write something to be published? I could just write something for my own interest and leave it in a bottom drawer.

Demon: Every writer wants to be published, to share it with others. But even if you do get published, you might be a failure, or at best, only mediocre.

Me: Maybe I should take the risk. Maybe it's okay to be mediocre.

Demon: Don't be silly, you were never allowed to be mediocre when you were growing up. Give up and stick to what you know. Your father told you that you couldn't write creatively, only factually.

Me: Leave my father out of this! He was far too critical. I'm sick of trying to prove to him I'm okay. You remind me of him a lot. He's dead now, so give me a break.

Demon: Now just consider what you're writing about. You must be stark, raving mad to write about that affair you had in Paris. A married man, how shameful, fancy telling the whole world about it! And what about 'Philippe' and his family, what would they think?

Me: Well, I'll camouflage it. I'll change the names, events and the place where we worked.

Demon: It won't ring true unless you write what you really know about. This story only works because you can still remember some of it.

Me: Well, why don't I just write it all down and then worry later what to do with it? Maybe it'll be a kind of memoir. Maybe it will turn into a semi-autobiographical novel about a young woman leaving Australia and growing up, finding out who she is by being so far away and having all those experiences. Then she returns as a different person.

Demon: It's very hard to write a novel. You need to know about plot and character and all sorts of technical things – why take on something so ambitious which is bound to fail?

Me: Well, I could try – I'll just do it chapter by chapter. You never get anywhere in life if you don't take some risks.

Demon: Why not go back to what you know, all that left brain stuff you can do well. It's much easier and you'll be happier.

Me: Why can't I do both – some creative writing and some work in the 'outer' world?

Demon: That won't happen. You work best when you're totally focussed on a project, not trying to do several things at once. Besides, you were offered that government project the other day and you turned it down. It would have been easy, but you thought it would interfere with your writing.

Me: Well, Barbara said you can do both writing and outside work. She does writing and teaching.

Demon: Can't you see this creative writing is just lonely and isolating? Look at you here, shut away in your room like a hermit. Why do you keep looking backwards? Get on with living in the present.

Me: I know it's lonely. I'll just have to balance it by seeing more of my friends and other people in between the writing.

Demon: You should be out in the world trying to help people. That's your duty, you know. Look at all the social problems there are. You should be ashamed to be just sitting here wallowing in this stuff.

Me: Well, I spent years trying to help 'change the world' and all I learned is that it's bloody hard. I'm taking a break from all that. Anyway, who is to say this sort of writing doesn't help anyone? Perhaps in a funny way it does. Perhaps it helps us understand how other people feel.

Demon: Oh yeah, tell that to a starving child in Africa.

Me: Piss off, you horrible demon! I'm not ready to give up. I like writing and there's something here I need to keep doing. I don't know why I need to, but I do. Most days it seems difficult and I can't write anything. But when it works, it feels very good and I go into such a deep concentration that I can't hear you. I hate you, you're evil. I'm not going to let you sabotage me. *Now go away!!*

I looked at the door to the bedroom and imagined slamming it shut in his face. I got up and made a mug of tea and took it back to the computer. I wondered how to beat the demon. Then it occurred to me that it would be easier if I stopped writing the story as a memoir and wrote it as a novel. That would allow me to change the time-frame for a start. Anna could arrive in Paris in September after the university vacation and stay for a year. I could leave out the three months in Turkey and the six months in New York. Perhaps the title of the novel would be, *A Year in Paris*.

With a novel, I thought, you can change anything. I would not have Philippe's wife working in the same building. Anna would know very little about her, but would be introduced to her some months later and the meeting would be dramatic. Maybe it would be at the office Christmas Party. I started to imagine how this would be, and decided it was fun to create something new.

As I thought about turning the memoir into a novel, I decided to change everything from the first person into the third person. It was easier to write 'Anna thought' and 'Anna said,' than 'I thought' and 'I said.' It helped to distance me further. I could also remove a lot of people and events which were not central to the story. I could leave out the two friends who shared my little apartment above the Flore. If Anna had a room of her own she could meet Philippe there each weekend, instead of in a hotel. Maybe I could call the book, *A Room Above the Café de Flore*. Yes, I liked that.

I read over what I'd written about Anna and Philippe working together and I started to rewrite it. I took them out of the office and into a café on the Seine, looking towards the Ile St Louis, where they talked about art and architecture. In the next scene I had them visit the Sorbonne, so that Philippe could show Anna the famous mural of Abélard teaching in the streets, in medieval Paris. I wanted Philippe to tell Anna the tragic love story of Abélard, who became the tutor to Héloïse, the niece of the Canon of Notre Dame.

I looked up from the computer. The writing was flowing again and I was going with it. Writing in the third person was helping me to go deeper into the scenes and to describe everything in more detail. I had never been inside the Sorbonne and had only seen the mural in a book, but it didn't matter, I could check the details later. I knew that I wanted Anna to be swept away by the story and to identify with the young Héloïse falling for her teacher. It would lead to the first kiss between Anna and Philippe.

When I finished writing that day, I was in a daze. That evening, I thought about my story and I was still thinking about it the next morning when I took my shower and had breakfast. Ideas and sentences kept popping into my head. When I sat down at the computer a few days later, I was ready to write about Anna and Philippe's first night together. Soon I was in the same dream-like state I had been in at Queenscliff and the story was writing itself. It was a tender love scene and I felt excited as I wrote it. When I had finished, I read it over and thought, '*What a bodice ripper!*' and laughed. I didn't know if I would ever be brave enough to show it to anyone, but I had fought off the demon, at least for the moment.

A few weeks later I emailed Barbara and told her what I was trying to do. I mentioned that I'd been writing my story as a memoir but was now trying it as fiction, in the third person, as a way of distancing myself.

'I'm so glad to hear you're still writing,' she replied. 'It's a good idea to try both memoir and fiction, but there's a big difference between the two. With memoir, the reader believes the story. *This is real*, they say, *this really happened*. But a novel works only with reference to itself. Nothing is relevant or of interest because it really happened, because we have no idea whether it happened or not. Things are only relevant if they relate to the character getting what he or she wants and the rising action of the story. The novel's interest is generated by tension and conflict, and those smaller and greater tensions are resolved as part of a complex whole.'

I read on. 'You will not be able to solve the problems in a memoir simply by writing about these things as though they were a novel,' she wrote, 'if you switch to fiction you will simply be creating a very complicated new set of problems. However, if you find it easier to write it in the third person, you could do so and then later on, turn it back into the first person.'

I read this twice and thought about it carefully. Then I decided to do the only thing that would allow me to keep writing. I would continue in the third person until I had finished a first draft, and worry later about whether it worked as an autobiographical novel or should be turned back into memoir.

7

Religion

'I thought about how my inner life and creativity had been driven underground. I wondered how this had happened. My loss of religion was one place to start.'

A few days later I sat at my desk and searched the Internet for 'left brain, right brain.' I wanted to understand why I had become so focused on logical, left-brain thinking throughout my life.

'*The left brain is logical, rational, analytical and objective,*' I read. '*It looks at the pieces and then puts them together to get the whole picture.*' Yes, I thought, that's how I'd always gone about a major piece of writing in the past. Whether it was an article, a submission or a book, I always did the research first, made a detailed plan and then did the writing. It was how I was taught to do essays in school.

I read on. '*The right brain is more intuitive, random and subjective. It sees the whole picture first and the details second. The right brain is more creative, but there's no right or wrong, it's merely two different ways of thinking.*'

I thought about how Race went about writing his articles and books. He would start by doing some reading and then write a few paragraphs. Then he would do some more research and write a bit more. His approach was the opposite of mine. He would start from the centre and work his way out, like a spiral. Whenever he complained that he was stuck with his writing, I would urge him to finish all the research first and make a plan. Each time he would smile patiently and say gently, 'I'm afraid I can't work like that. I work out what I want to say as I go along.'

I had never understood his method before. Now I realised that it was more intuitive, and it was the way I was now starting to write. I was working out what my novel was about as I went along. I had a vague path to follow, based on what had happened when I was a young woman, but I had no plans for what to put in or to leave out or how to structure each chapter. The chapters were emerging as I went along. The writing was throwing up problems, but in a mysterious way, solutions were appearing too. My training as a journalist and a lifetime of reading books were serving me well.

I was finding that each chapter had an optimal length. I would put things in and take them out, like packing a suitcase. Not too light and not too heavy. Each chapter had to move the story forward with dramatic action and lively dialogue, and it needed a beginning, middle and end. Sometimes my characters got what they wanted, but then found out it was not what they expected. I was realising that the ending of each chapter was very important. It had to have a twist or throw up a new question or problem, or throw out a life-raft to the next chapter. All this was a new way of writing for me and it was liberating.

I rushed into Race's study to tell him that at last I

understood his method and that it was creative and intuitive. 'Well, that sounds good,' he said, 'but I wish it wasn't so damned difficult. I've just spent the past hour trying to get one paragraph right.'

I smiled. 'I do that too. Sometimes the writing comes in a spurt and other times it dries up completely. Some days I write a whole scene without stopping, but then I spend days and days fiddling around with it, word by word.'

'Some days I can't write at all,' he said, 'I'm completely blocked.'

'That's part of the process,' I said. I went into my study and came back with a copy of Thomas Moore's *Care of the Soul*, which I had been reading. I found the passage I wanted and read it out. *'Creative work can be exciting, inspiring and godlike, but it is also quotidian, humdrum and full of anxieties, frustrations, dead ends, mistakes and failures.'*

'Perhaps we're just masochists,' he said.

I smiled and went back to my desk and looked again at the entry on left brain, right brain. *'Schools tend to favour left-brain modes of thinking,'* it said, *'while downplaying the right-brain ones. Left-brain scholastic subjects focus on logical thinking, analysis and accuracy. Right-brain subjects focus on aesthetics, feeling and creativity.'* I thought about the schools I had attended. Yes, it was true. There was no encouragement of creative writing and I was made to give up art classes which I loved, when they clashed with an academic subject. I remembered that on weekends I liked to read in bed in the mornings, but my father said I was lazy and made me get up and do something 'useful' like raking leaves in the garden. Idleness and daydreaming were frowned on.

I opened a new page on the computer and started writing about this. Soon I was deep in concentration and all of a sudden the screen went blank. The computer seemed to have turned itself off. I jabbed desperately at the start button and it came to life again, but I hadn't saved the document and there was not a word left. I stared at the screen and burst out laughing. What blatant sabotage! My 'father' had put a stop to those thoughts, just as he tried to put a stop to any ideas of mine which were not provable or which he did not agree with. I was amazed at the power of my subconscious.

I decided to give up writing for the day and set out for a walk on the river near our house. It was a beautiful November day, warm and still, and it raised my spirits. The sun was so bright on the water that it hurt my eyes, like a flash from an oxy-acetylene torch. As I walked, I listened to Vivaldi on my headphones, and as the choir swelled into '*Gloria in Excelsis Deo*,' I felt a burst of happiness. I reflected on my good fortune, to be out walking while others were at work, and to be given this time for writing and reflection.

When I came to the bend in the river I stopped to lean on the fence and look down through the yellow gorse bushes that clung to the banks. Some leaves were floating slowly down towards the sea and it was mesmerising to watch them drifting, drifting on the muddy water. I thought about how my inner life and creativity had been driven underground. I wondered how this had happened. My loss of religion was one place to start.

As a child, I was quite involved in the church. My mother came from a strong Presbyterian family and brought us up in her faith, although my father was not religious. We went to Presbyterian schools and to church on Sunday mornings. The church was about a mile from our house and we walked there to Sunday school, my brother, sister and I. A few blocks before the church there was a small corner store where you could buy sweets and ice creams. My brother, always a rebel, used to stop there and buy lollies with the money we had been given to put in the collection plate. My sister and I wrestled with this temptation and resisted. After a while my brother simply stopped coming altogether.

Sunday school was held in the hall opposite the church. We sat in a small circle around the teacher who was a nice, quiet man. When he told us about Jesus being crucified on the cross, I wanted to know more.

'Do you mean they put nails through his hands?' I asked.

'Yes,' said the teacher, 'and hung him on the cross to die.'

'Do you mean they put nails right through his hands, with a hammer or something?'

The teacher seemed a bit uncomfortable and said, 'Well, I don't know exactly how they did it.' The other kids were not asking questions, but I needed to know.

'How long did it take him to die like that?' I asked. 'It would be really painful, wouldn't it?' I wondered why the teacher wasn't upset. I wanted to know more, but the teacher didn't want to say. Perhaps he didn't know. It was very disappointing. We were told that it was really important, that Jesus died on the cross for us, to save us, and yet they couldn't tell us much about what happened at all.

'Well children,' he said cheerily, 'I think we can leave that for today. Get out your picture books and colour in the lovely picture of Christ with his disciples.'

After Sunday school we joined my mother for the church service. My sister and I found it long and boring, but I liked the hymns, the peaceful atmosphere and the light filtering through the long church windows. My mother took great care about our clothes for church. Once she made my sister and me matching linen dresses. Mine was pale blue and my sister's was lemon. They had 'peter pan' collars, little buttons down the front, and a gathered skirt. We wore long white socks and shiny black patent leather shoes. Our straight blonde hair was tied to one side with a ribbon that matched the dress.

When I was about ten, a girl called Ruby Davidson invited some of us to her house after school for a children's group called 'Crusaders.' It was fun and I went every week. When we arrived, her parents gave us cordial and biscuits and then we had games in the front garden, playing in teams. After that we went into the front room where they told us bible stories and we played more games.

Ruby's parents were not like mine. Mrs Davidson did not wear lipstick or go to the hairdresser like my mother. She wore very plain clothes and she looked rather mouse-like with straight wispy hair. She was quite small, while Mr Davidson was very tall and had dark bushy eyebrows and a hollow-cheeked face. The other kids said they were Methodists and didn't drink alcohol or go to parties.

When the summer holidays came around my sister and I went to a Crusader holiday camp. We stayed in an old house near the sea and had mystery chases where we followed clues from the bible hidden around the house and garden. In the evening we were allowed to spend our pocket money on lollies and to buy special books. I fell in love with *Mary Jones and her Bible*, about a Welsh girl who wanted a bible but had no money. She was so poor she went barefoot everywhere, but by walking for miles and doing odd jobs for people she saved up, penny by penny, until she achieved her heart's desire and bought a bible.

I also devoured the 'Jungle Doctor' books, about a missionary doctor deep in the African jungle. With a team of loyal black assistants he saved lives and served God. The natives were primitive and followed the witch doctors. When a baby was sick, the 'cure' was for an old crone to take some urine and scratch it onto the back of the baby's throat with her long, dirty finger nail. The Jungle Doctor taught them hygiene and saved their souls as well as their bodies. I decided right then that I was going to be a missionary when I grew up.

When I came home from the camp I was in a state of excitement and was determined to read a verse from the bible each day, as the camp leaders had suggested. They had given us a list of readings, and as soon as I woke, I dressed quietly so as not to wake my sister, and crept down the stairs and into the garden with my bible in my hand.

It was summer holidays, and although it was early morning, the garden was already warm and light, the sun filtering through the large oak trees that spread over the front lawn. I crossed the soft grass to the swing that hung on the oak tree nearest the house. I sat on the swing and opened my bible and read the marked passage. It was Matthew 19:19, 'Honour your father and mother, and you shall love your neighbour as yourself.'

At the Crusader camp they had told us to think about what we read in the bible and to pray for a few minutes, to feel at one with God. I thought about my parents. I loved and respected them and was happy to honour them. Then I thought about my neighbours. The Jones family were easy to love. They were kind and friendly and my sister and I were frequent visitors to their house. But I didn't like our other neighbours, the Hatch family, nearly as much. Mr Hatch was a bit scary and the family kept to themselves.

I held onto the swing and shut my eyes tight and prayed to God to help me feel better towards the Hatch family and to love all my neighbours as myself. I felt the sun on my back, the warm smell of the garden and the bible in my hands. Everything was quiet, apart from the sound of birds in the oak trees and a car starting up in the street outside. I thought about goodness and love and how I wanted to help people when I grew up, like the Jungle Doctor.

I opened my eyes and looked around me, at the loveliness of the garden and the big house, silent and unmoving. I loved being alone like this. A few feet away, our black and white collie dog was sprawled in the sun nuzzling his nose into his long fur. I felt happiness sweep through me, and looked up into the tree above the swing, with its umbrella of green leaves and its rough black trunk. Across the lawn my mother's flower-bed was a blaze of colour with roses, azaleas, poppies, hydrangeas and stocks. I grasped the ropes firmly, lifted my feet off the ground and swung myself up, back and forth, gathering speed, higher and higher.

I was always a happy child, but on those mornings on the swing I discovered what Bliss was, and believed I was close to God. If my parents thought I was becoming overly religious, they said nothing to me. Perhaps it was just a phase, because by the end of the summer I had given up the bible readings and I no longer thought about being a missionary. But I kept my desire to help people.

A few years later, when I was about thirteen, I asked my father why he didn't come to church with us. We were sitting at the dinner table and when I asked the question, there was a sudden silence. My father looked at my mother and she looked at him, saying nothing. Then, still looking at him, she nodded. My father turned to me and said, 'I'll talk to you after dinner.' I felt very important.

Later that evening we went into the room we called the Den which looked out on the back garden. My father stretched out on the window seat, a pillow behind his head, and I sat at the other end, at his feet. I looked at him and thought how handsome he was, with his light brown hair and blue eyes.

'When your mother and I married,' he said. 'We made a pact. She believed in religion and I didn't, so we decided that you children would be brought up her way, going to church and Sunday school until you were old enough to think for yourselves. Then you could decide whether you wanted to be religious or not. I've tried not to impose my views on any of you.'

'Why don't you come to church?' I asked. 'Why don't you believe in it?'

'You know my training is in Science and the Law,' he said. 'When you're a scientist you don't believe things unless they're proved to be true. You have a hypothesis, which is to say you have an idea about something, and you collect the evidence and test the hypothesis. If it's proved, then you know it's true.'

He looked at me intently. 'I'm an Atheist. I don't believe in God or religion. I believe religion is the opposite of truth, it's just superstition. It's what people make up in order to explain things that are a mystery to them. The idea that there's a God up in the sky, looking down on us, knowing everything we do and say and determining what happens, is just superstition.'

He put a cushion behind his back and went on. 'I don't believe that when we die we go to some place called heaven where angels play on harps, or we go to hell where we burn in fires. That's all made up. The reality is that when we die, our body rots and crumbles away until there's nothing left but the bones. We cease to exist. So what could go to heaven? We have no brain left, no body left, we simply cease to exist.'

I looked at him, trying to understand, full of confusion. 'But what about the Bible,' I said. 'It's all in the Bible.'

He sighed impatiently. 'The Bible was written by people who were religious. They believed in their religion, but most of what is in the Bible was invented, it wasn't true. Look at the story of the loaves and the fishes. Do you really think a few loaves and a few fishes could suddenly feed a large crowd of people?'

'I don't know,' I said in a small voice. 'Well, I suppose not.'

'All these miracles are just fairy stories,' he said. 'I know it's hard for you to think so, because you've been brought up to believe all this stuff. But you have to know sooner or later.'

'But God created the earth,' I said.

My father gave a short laugh and jumped up and paced about the room. He turned and looked down at me. 'That's the greatest rubbish of all,' he said. 'God created the earth in a week. What does that mean? You have to turn to Science to understand creation. It has all been proven beyond doubt, with proper, scientific proof. The fact is that millions of years ago, life began on earth with tiny living organisms evolving out of a swamp. They were made up of a combination of chemicals. Those tiny organisms eventually grew into bigger organisms. And over millions of years they evolved into animals and birds and plants and eventually into human beings. It was all explained by a scientist called Charles Darwin. He proved that over millions of years, living things evolved into humans. It had nothing to do with God.'

He sat down and paused while I struggled to understand all this. I loved my father and knew he was very clever. But I could not fit what he was saying with all that I had learned from school and church and Sunday school and Crusaders.

'But what about everything that's beautiful?' I said.

'What about flowers and sunsets and beautiful music. Is it all made up of chemicals?'

My father smiled. 'Well it's a bit more complicated than that. Take a rainbow for example. It certainly is beautiful but it's just the refraction of the light's rays into different colours due to the moisture in the air. Anything can be explained scientifically if you analyse it carefully enough.'

I tried a few more questions, but he had an answer every time. My old world was crumbling. I felt sad about it, but proud that my father thought I was old enough to be talking to me like this, like an adult. Somewhere in the house I heard my sister playing her recorder and my mother rattled something in the kitchen. My father started speaking again.

'What I hate about religion,' he said, 'is the power of the churches. They've been a force of evil down the ages. They meddle in people's lives and persecute people who don't follow their particular brand of religion. They teach a lot of dangerous rubbish.'

'Take their attitude to sex, for example. The churches have done tremendous damage by teaching people that sex is evil, or that it should be avoided unless you're married. Some churches teach that contraception is wicked and must be forbidden, and then people who are poor go on having large families which they can't support. A great deal of evil has been perpetrated in this world in the name of religion. When countries go to war they always say God is on their side. They never think he's on the other side, of course.'

He went on giving me examples throughout history of

the church persecuting, killing and inflicting misery on people in God's name. I felt overwhelmed by all the evidence he was piling up. 'But Dad,' I said, 'doesn't the church do good things too? It teaches us to lead a good life and look after others.'

He looked at me sternly. 'You don't need religion in order to lead a good life. I've thought about this deeply and read the views of many philosophers and thinkers. I try to be a useful member of society and to contribute more than I receive. I believe in honesty and trustworthiness. I try to be kind to others and to be responsible, especially to my family and my business partners. I try to see the other person's point of view, even when it's diametrically opposed to mine. We should all strive to live an ethical life, but we don't need religion to tell us how to do it.'

He stood up again and ran his hand though his hair. 'I hate religion,' he said. 'But you must realise that we live in a society where the churches are powerful and hard to avoid. I've suffered all my life because I don't believe. I hate being hypocritical, but I have to be sometimes. I didn't want to be married in a church, but your mother and her family would not tolerate a wedding anywhere else. I go along with it at your school too. As chairman of the school council I have to go to the speech nights and church ceremonies and put up with the prayers and the references to God. I hold my tongue and say nothing and you will have to as well if you want to get on in this world.'

I was silent. Everything he said seemed so logical. I had no more arguments to put up. And yet, part of me felt it could not be this simple, this black and white. I found it hard to believe that everything could be explained by chemicals and molecules. I went to find my mother. She was in the laundry, sorting the washing.

'Oh there you are,' she said. 'You can help me fold the sheets.' She took a large white cotton sheet and gave me two corners to hold, one in each hand. I stepped back until the sheet was stretched out between my hands and hers, and we shook it up and down. Then, carefully, as she had taught me, I folded one side over at the same time as she did, and then again, until it was a slim, straight line. She tucked her end under her chin, took my end and folded the sheet quickly into a neat square and smoothed it out on the table with her hands. Then she handed me the next sheet.

'Mum,' I said, 'Dad says religion is all rubbish, but you don't think it is, do you?'

She laughed. 'Don't worry about him,' she said. 'He takes everything too seriously.'

'But Mum, why do you believe in God?'

My mother put the sheet down slowly, thinking. 'Well, I don't know exactly whether there's a God or not,' she said, 'but when I'm in trouble I pray to Him. When I had your brother I got pneumonia and they thought I was going to die, and I prayed to God to let me live. It was very comforting. I can't really explain it any other way.' I looked at her, thinking about what Dad had said and what she had said.

'Let's go and have some cocoa,' she said, 'and then it really is time for you to go to bed.'

Some time after that evening I stopped going to church

and Sunday school. I could no longer believe in a God with a white beard sitting up in the sky or in praying to him. When I was fifteen and changed schools, I decided not to close my eyes and say the Lord's Prayer at assembly each morning. It seemed hypocritical to do so if I did not believe. I sang the hymns though, because I loved the music.

With my girl friends, sometimes late at night I'd raise the question of religion and ask if they believed or not. They said they didn't know. I reasoned with them the way my father had reasoned with me, and they agreed that it was all probably made up, but they didn't seem to care the way I did. It was the first real intellectual problem I'd grappled with. I couldn't fault my father's logic, but part of me wondered if Science really did have all the answers, or whether some things were just a mystery.

As an adult, when I was asked, I'd say I was an agnostic, not an atheist. And sometimes I would experience again that moment of Bliss I had as a small child in the garden, on the swing. One night in London, walking home from a party, along Regent's Canal, I saw the moon reflected on the water through the trees and was seized with a moment of pure beauty and pure happiness. There were several more moments like that, always unexpected.

Now, at fifty-eight, I thought about all this as I walked by the river. My father did his job well; he trained me to be a good citizen and to think logically. That was invaluable in journalism and later as an advocate. I could never make an assertion in an article or a submission without feeling him looking over my shoulder saying, *'can you prove it?'*

I became good at left-brain activities, but at a price. Now I was fortunate in being able to redress the balance, to try my hand at something more creative and to pass my time in idleness and day-dreaming without feeling guilty.

I suddenly felt love and compassion for my father. He was a complex, sensitive man who was forced by his upbringing to try to crush his feminine side. I reflected that as I got older, I felt more tolerant towards other people's beliefs, as long as they did not hurt others. In regard to religion, I felt that my father's viewpoint was too angry and too narrow.

In his relentless drive for logic, his need to drive out all uncertainty, he missed the point. The point was not whether there was a God or not, but how to conceptualise the mystery of life, the things that cannot be explained, the life force. The point was how to explain the existence of abstract things like beauty and love and life and goodness and eternity, or perhaps not to explain them at all. And whether we are poorer, as I think my father was, if we crush all thoughts that are not logical, scientific and easily provable.

8

Talya returns

'My newfound happiness was based on surprises I could not have guessed at a few months earlier.'

As Christmas approached I started to get excited about my daughter's return to Melbourne, but also rather apprehensive. Would she be distant, the way she'd been on some of her earlier visits, or would we become closer now she was pregnant?

Until she was sixteen, ten years earlier, we had been very close. Talya and I looked alike, we were alike in many ways, and when she was growing up my friends jokingly called her my 'clone.' At sixteen she went to France on an exchange scholarship, spurred on probably by my stories of living in Paris as a young woman. I missed her terribly and went to French classes each week, getting ready to join her when the exchange finished. I flew to Paris, went to the student hostel where we'd arranged to meet, and waited in the lobby.

It was late afternoon and there were not many people around. I waited and waited. Then I became worried. I had no phone number for her and no idea where she was. Finally she arrived on the back of a large motorbike. She strode towards me, taller and more beautiful than before, blonde hair streaming behind her. She kissed me coolly on both cheeks and said, 'Sorry we're late Mum.' Then she glanced at the tall, handsome Frenchman getting off the motorbike and said, 'This is Paul,' pronouncing it *'Pol'* in the French way.

I looked at her in amazement, registering that she was no longer a child. She said, 'I'm staying at Paul's place tonight. I won't be staying at your hotel, but we'd like to have dinner with you.' I was filled with shock and rejection, but did as I was told. We had a pleasant dinner, and by ten p.m. I was back in my hotel room, weeping into the telephone to Race, 12,000 miles away. 'She doesn't want me anymore,' I sobbed, while he tried to be supportive and reminded me that he'd be with us in a few days.

We'd planned a family holiday with her in the French countryside and in the end Paul came too. He was ten years older than Talya, a nice post-graduate student, as bemused by her seeming toughness and confidence as we were. One day, walking through the fields, a farmer asked if they'd like to buy one of his barns and convert it into a cottage. They liked being taken for a young couple.

Then came the next bombshell – she'd decided that when we returned to Melbourne she'd leave school, get a job and move out of home. We were devastated. She was intelligent, she'd done well at school, and we couldn't understand her decision. We'd always stressed the importance of education and of getting qualifications in order to have interesting, well-paid work. We spent the holiday trying to reason with her. We brought out the usual parental armoury – bribes, threats, tears (on my part) anger, reason and despair; all to no avail.

We returned to Melbourne and she went back to school reluctantly. The following year when she was seventeen, she left school and got a job as a trainee receptionist and moved out of home. We said, in anger and sorrow, that we'd support her if she was studying, but otherwise she'd have to support herself. She said she would, and stuck to it bravely.

I talked to my parents, weeping again. My mother said Talya was headstrong and we should have been stricter with her. My father, gentle and sympathetic, said Talya had decided to take on the whole world, and because the world was a big place, she'd find that it would kick her in the shins quite often. He was right. I was surprised by how much he'd mellowed with age. When I was growing up he was strict about everything, especially our education, but with his grandchildren he was extremely tolerant. He told Talya that he admired her adventurousness. He said all his life he'd conformed to society's expectations and part of him wished he'd been a bit more daring.

When Talya decided to leave home, her brother Keir, two years older, moved out with her. I watched as they embarked on a life that was difficult and sometimes risky, but in their eyes fun and liberating. They lived in a variety of run-down houses with other young people and finished their schooling at the Council of Adult Education. Race and I were there when they needed us, but I learned painfully there was not much I could do to help them. It was a journey they had to make on their own. I wondered how much it was a reaction against us. We valued hard work, education, qualifications, achievements, public service and serious-mindedness. Perhaps it was inevitable that they would reject all that for a while.

At nineteen, Talya went to Japan to teach English and stayed there on and off for several years. She used it as a base from which to save money and travel the world. She worked in a variety of jobs and had numerous boyfriends. She told us she wanted to live life to the full and try every experience. We kept in touch with regular emails and phone calls and sensed that she told us only a fraction of what was happening, just as I had done with my parents in my twenties.

When we met up with her again at intermittent inter-vals, her guard was up. As the years went by, I felt as though part of my heart was missing. Then, out of the blue, she sent an email saying she was tired of living the life of a gypsy and had decided to return home and go to university, possibly in Queensland. She flew back and drove up the coast with Race, looking at every university along the way. She returned to Japan to save money and pack up her life there, intending to enrol the following year.

Then in October, just after I had returned from my writing course at Queenscliff, I received an email saying she was pregnant and was going to keep the baby. I clicked it open one day sitting at my desk and read it in amaze-ment. She said she would be a single mother and live in Melbourne. She did not want any financial help from us, but would value our help in other ways if we felt able to give it. We were invited to help with the child '*morally, physically and spiritually.*' The tone was cool, determined and independent.

As soon as I had finished reading the email I ran out to the garden where Race was tying a creeper to the fence. '*Talya's going to have a baby*,' I screamed. He stared at me in disbelief. Finally he said, 'What about university?'

'I guess that's postponed.'

We went inside and I read out the email. Then we discussed how to handle it. She was always very determined and had made it clear that she'd go ahead with or without our help. We decided to be very positive. We phoned and congratulated her and said we would help in whatever way we could. We told her we were delighted she was coming back to Melbourne and the family.

Her relief on the phone was palpable. She apologised for criticising me in recent emails. She said she was afraid to tell me about the baby because she thought I'd try to talk her out of it, but now that I had accepted the news, she was looking forward to giving me a new grandchild. I knew that I would be more involved with this one, because Talya was doing it alone and because now I had more time.

We asked about the father and she said it was a Melbourne guy she'd met in Japan, where they had a brief romance. His name was Javier, she said, pronouncing it *Havier*. She said his parents were Spanish, but he grew up in Melbourne. He was back in Australia now and they were still friends, but they didn't intend to live together. When I hung up the phone it struck me that this conversation was a watershed moment. I felt that from now on she and I were pulling together, instead of apart.

The next night Race and I had dinner in a Lebanese restaurant in Carlton and discussed our impending grand-parenting role. I said this time I wanted him to share the responsibility, since he was semi-retired. I didn't want to do it alone, as I had in the past. He agreed readily. A couple at the next table had a small baby sleeping in a capsule and we kept sneaking glances at it, wondering if Talya's baby would be like that. Race joked that he would take the baby in a capsule to meetings. We were in it together and I sensed there would be lots of joy. I imagined us pushing a pram along the beach or in a park.

Talya told her older brothers and sisters, who swallowed their surprise and agreed to give support. We were all taking time to get used to the news. Our son-in-law John summed it up when he said, 'It's a dramatic way for Talya to re-enter the family.' She sent daily emails bubbling over with excitement about the pregnancy and her return to Melbourne. Her brothers and sisters emailed back and started collecting baby clothes.

She emailed that Javier was still in shock about the pregnancy but had offered to help. 'At this stage I'm glad I don't have a partner,' she wrote. 'Relationships are hard. I haven't been very good at them so far. At least this way I can bring up the baby the way I want, without having to consider someone else's views all the time. Maybe I'll find someone later, I don't know. I'm not thinking about that now.'

I sensed now that I was talking to an adult, and that her decisions were valid for her and not for me to comment on, except to give support. We were back to the closeness we had before she went to France at sixteen. I thought of the counsellor who said she rebelled against that closeness and had to get away from it in order to find her own identity, and that she would come back to me when she had children of her own.

Soon she was on her way home, travelling through Laos and Cambodia. I emailed that I would love to see those countries and she replied, 'You have us any time you want, I'm sure the baby will love travel as much as you and I do.' I read it and thought, is this the same person who pushed me away for so long and caused me such pain? I loved the idea that Race and I might travel with her and the child one day, and reflected that life was full of the most amazing surprises.

So now it was time to tell my mother. I waited until my next visit, when we were having afternoon tea in her bedroom at the retirement home. She'd been out of hospital for a while and was almost back to her old self, dressed stylishly in black pants and a red silk shirt with a gold necklace. She'd been to the hairdresser that morning and her nails were freshly painted to match her shirt. The garden outside was bright with sunshine and I could smell jasmine through the window.

'You're looking good, Mum,' I said. 'No more Greek dancing I hope.'

She giggled. She'd recently had another fall while showing some of the other old ladies how to do 'Zorba the Greek.'

'No, but I joined in carpet bowls yesterday, very carefully.'

'Is the physio still coming?'

'Yes, twice a week. She's giving me exercises and I'm not allowed to go anywhere without this.' She touched the walking frame beside her.

'That's good. Be sure to use it when you go to the bathroom in the middle of the night.' I looked at the walking frame. It was cleverly designed so she could lean on the handles while she walked, but when she was tired she could turn it round and sit down on it like a chair. I lifted the padded seat to see what she had in the basket underneath. There was a romance novel, a clean handkerchief and a bottle of gin. I laughed and held up the bottle.

'That's for drinks before dinner,' she said. 'I meet my friends in the lounge room at six o'clock.' She leaned forward and lowered her voice. 'I'm not like Mavis next door; she carries sherry in hers and asks you to have a drink with her in the middle of the morning.'

'Well at least you won't get caught for drink driving.'

We smiled at each other and she offered me some shortbread. She was in such a good mood I decided to plunge in.

'I've got some news,' I said. 'Talya's coming back for Christmas.'

'Oh, that's lovely dear, just for a visit?'

'No, she's coming back for good.'

'For good?' She stopped fussing with the tea cups.

'Mum, there's something I have to tell you. She's pregnant. The baby's due in April. She's decided to go ahead with it.'

'What? But she's not married. Who's the father?'

'He's a Melbourne guy, of Spanish background. She met him in Tokyo and they had a brief romance, but they didn't expect this to happen.'

Mum sniffed. 'Well she must have done it to trick the father into marrying her.'

'No, it wasn't like that at all. She doesn't want to marry him. They don't want to live together. She's decided to be a single mother.'

'Typical of a man,' said Mum. 'They have five minutes of fun and don't want the responsibility.'

'It's not like that. He sounds like a responsible guy. Look, we were stunned when we heard, but it's her decision, not ours. She's an adult and she'll be all right. Race and I will help her and the rest of the family will too. She'll stay with us until she gets a place of her own. Things have changed since your day. It's not a scandal any more to be a single mother.'

She looked at me intently. 'You watch out. You'll find she likes the baby at first, but then she'll get sick of it and dump it on you, and you'll be left to bring it up. You shouldn't get too involved. You have your own life to lead.'

I stared at her in amazement. I found her statement outrageous and an insult to Talya, but I took a deep breath and said, 'I don't think that will happen.' I suddenly realised that Mum was afraid I'd have my attention diverted to the baby and away from her. She had become used to me always being available, just around the corner. After all, I'd looked after her for the past six years since my father died.

'I'll still have time for you,' I said. 'I can help Talya and you too, you know. It's a good thing I'm not working full time any more, isn't it?' She looked doubtful.

I went home and continued cleaning out the second bedroom, getting it ready for Talya. I moved out my laptop and files and reflected that I wouldn't be doing much writing for a while, but it didn't matter. I was looking forward to the Christmas break when I could help Talya and catch up with our family and friends.

She flew in three days before Christmas, looking wonderful in a loose fitting Indian top and pants. She hugged us both and as soon as we were home, excitedly unpacked and distributed presents. She handed me a beautiful silk scarf in the blues and pinks I like, Race received a CD of *Madam Butterfly* and she laid out presents for her older brothers and sisters and her six nieces and nephews.

When our son Keir arrived for dinner that night, we celebrated her return and she told us about her travels. Then Keir asked about Javier. She said he was very good looking and had qualities she felt she lacked, like being artistic and entrepreneurial. I looked at my tall son and daughter talking quietly together and reflected that my life had come full circle. They were home once more, but this time as adults.

On Christmas day I woke to hear Talya singing as she went into the bathroom. There was no sign now of the rebellious teenager. It was the best Christmas present I could have had. At Christmas lunch she was the centre of attention, serene and happy in a sleeveless black maternity dress with her long hair tied back in a bun. I helped my mother walk to the table and was pleased that she did not refer to the pregnancy and kept her views to herself about her impending great-grandchild.

Throughout the day my children and step-children and their partners helped with the food and the cleaning up, and I reflected that at last I could take a back seat after years of organising family events. It was another milestone. I said to Race that night, 'I'm redundant now. If I was run over by a bus they'd take over these family gatherings effortlessly.' It was a comforting thought.

In the next few weeks I often accompanied Talya as she drove around looking at places to rent. Finally, she chose a flat in East Brighton, about twenty minutes drive from our house. It needed some work and we embarked on a family project of fixing it up. Talya painted and shopped for furniture while I made curtains for each room. Race did some painting and later helped with the move.

I still visited my mother twice a week and told her what was happening. It amused me that she had not told anybody in her retirement home about Talya, because it was too shocking. But she seemed to have softened somewhat about the pregnancy and when I told her Talya was looking for a cheap second hand car, she wrote out a cheque to contribute towards it.

In mid-January Race and I went to stay with friends at Bell's Beach, south-west of Melbourne. On the first morning I woke early and took a mug of tea back to bed. I pushed an extra pillow behind my back and sat there nursing the tea, looking out past the veranda and the fields to the sea. It was already a dazzling blue and it looked like a good day for a swim.

I felt a surge of pure happiness as I always do when I arrive at that beautiful place, far from the city and responsibilities. I looked down at Race sleeping beside me and placed my hand on his bare shoulder, feeling the warmth. It struck me that my hand, with its gold wedding ring, had been touching that same skin for nearly thirty years. He turned and smiled sleepily. I said, 'what more could

I want? I'm here in the most comfortable bed in the world, with this view, you beside me and the whole day to enjoy.'

He moved in the bed, thinking of an answer and I said, 'Don't tell me there are problems out in the world waiting to be fixed, because I don't want to know about them.' He laughed and snuggled closer while I sipped my tea and looked out dreamily, smiling with contentment. I had just turned fifty-nine and my writing was on hold, but everything in my life was going well. I'd learned to treasure such moments, knowing they were transient. Life was a roller coaster and when the good times came you had to stop and look around, sniff the air and make the most of every minute.

I reflected that my newfound happiness was based on surprises I could not have guessed at a few months earlier. The night before, friends had asked about my plans for the coming year. I said I'd given up my job and would be completely free now to help Talya and the new baby, to get on with my writing and to continue helping my mother. They did not know what pleasure it gave me to say those few words, to be able to see the way ahead at last.

I thought about the writing. It had taken me years of false starts and detours to get to the point where I could say with some confidence that it was what I expected to be doing for the next period of my life. It was only by cutting back my work and stepping into a vacuum, that I had slowly, painfully and confusedly stumbled into my writing and a completely new way of looking at the world.

By shedding much of what seemed important in the busy outer world, I'd discovered an inner world around a core of peace and stillness. I'd discovered that you had to leave the ground fallow for some time before creativity emerged. I'd begun to see the world through new glasses, divided into those who'd discovered this secret world of peace and harmony and those who had not. It seemed to me that some people resisted the pull as hard as they could. Now, as I lay in bed looking out to the sea, it felt like a small miracle just to know what I wanted to do. I wanted to go on writing the story of my earlier life in Paris and intended to get back to it as soon as Talya was settled.

In early February I had a surprise job offer. I went with Race to hear a lecture on social entrepreneurship. We'd read about this 'third way' in Britain and were interested in how it could be implemented in Australia. It had similarities to the 'local empowerment' I had observed when working in regional development. After the lecture, a friend who was in publishing asked if I would like to write a book on the subject. A few years earlier I might have been excited by this offer, but now I could only shake my head and say no. She looked surprised and said, 'But this book will put you back on the map as a writer.'

'I don't care about the map anymore,' I said. 'I just want to do my creative writing and help my daughter and my mother.'

By mid February Talya was six months pregnant and her flat was nearly ready to move into. I went into her room at our house one night with some washing, and found her lying on her back with her hands stretched out on the large oval of her stomach. She turned her head to me, smiled dreamily and said, 'It's moving Mum, feel it.' I placed my hand on her belly and waited. There was a little flutter beneath my fingers and then an upheaval, a kick or maybe a somersault.

'What was that?' I said, laughing.

'It gets really active at this time of night. In fact it hardly seems to sleep at all, day or night. A friend of mine says if it doesn't sleep in the womb, it won't sleep much after it's born either.'

'Oh dear,' I said, remembering the sleepless nights I had when Talya was a baby. 'You'd better check that out with a few other people. Perhaps it's an old wives' tale.'

I sat on the bed and we chatted happily about what we would do the next day. It was fun doing things together, setting up the flat, shopping, sewing, pottering and enjoying the summer. I loved preparing the evening meal together, chatting at the dinner table and afterwards watching television with her or reading, when she was not catching up with her old friends. I knew I'd miss all this when she was gone, but at least now she would only be a short distance away, instead of on the other side of the world.

She had asked me and her older sister Vanessa to be her 'birth partners' at the hospital. I thought how different it would be for her than it was for me. When I gave birth to her and her brother, I had three stepchildren at home and Race was in Canberra most of the time as a member of parliament. She did not have a partner the way I did, but she had us and her older brothers and sisters and their partners and children, who all lived in Melbourne and were rallying round with love and generosity.

They phoned her every few days and sometimes came over to help as she painted the flat. As they had all finished having babies, they had a lot of clothes, toys, cots, prams and furniture which they now passed on to her. Everyone talked endlessly and excitedly about the new baby. It had become a family project, a rallying point for all of us. I watched all this with joy. It seemed that Talya's return and the new baby was bringing our family closer together.

9

Caleb's birth

'Watching the birth of my grandchild was one of the greatest events of my life.'

The phone shrilled next to the bed and I fumbled for it in the dark. It was Talya.

'Sorry to wake you,' she said, 'but the contractions started before midnight and they've been regular since about two a.m. They're now about ten to fifteen minutes apart.' She sounded very calm.

'That's amazing,' I said. 'Something woke me about two a.m. and I've been lying here ever since, wondering if anything was happening. It must have been ESP. What time is it now?'

'Four a.m. I phoned the midwife at the hospital and she said we don't need to go until the contractions are about five minutes apart. That could be hours away.'

'Shall I come over now?'

'Yes, but there's no rush.'

I felt excited and relieved, because Talya was nine days overdue. It was early May and the baby had been due in April. She had stopped putting on weight and the doctor was worried that the baby might have stopped growing. A few days more and she would have to be induced. I turned to Race, who was awake and looking anxious. I explained what was happening, then kissed him and said, 'Try to go back to sleep. I'll phone you when there's more news.'

I showered and dressed quickly and packed a small bag with some sandwiches and a drink for the hospital. Soon I was in the car driving south towards Talya's place. The streets were dark and deserted. It felt strange, like the film *On the Beach* where Melbourne is the last refuge after a nuclear holocaust.

As I drove, I thought about the day before. We had celebrated my mother's ninety-fifth birthday in her retirement home with a large passionfruit sponge cake, her favourite. Talya had started having some irregular cramps during the day and the midwife had said labour would probably begin within the next twenty-four hours. Vanessa and I, as the birth partners, were on standby. Vanessa, my-forty-year old stepdaughter, was a lawyer in a busy city practice and had warned her office that she'd be absent.

I let myself into Talya's flat and found her in her dressing gown, running a bath. 'The contractions are more frequent now,' she said, 'but fluctuating wildly.' She handed me a notepad on which she was keeping a record. The gap between contractions was irregular – seven minutes, six, eight, three, ten minutes. The length of each contraction varied from thirty seconds to one minute. I handed it back and said, 'Well, at last it's happening.' We smiled at each other.

While she had her bath, I made myself some tea and

wandered around the flat. It was in an old building but it faced north and was filled with light. She'd made it very cosy, with pictures on the walls and brightly coloured furniture from Ikea. The small second bedroom was all ready for the baby. There was a cot in the corner, a changing table and a large container for soiled nappies. A colourful mobile hung above the changing table and she'd pasted an animal frieze around the walls.

I heard her go into the bedroom and found her perched on the edge of the double bed, breathing deeply through a contraction. I crawled under the doona and we chatted quietly. Soon I started to feel sleepy and went into the lounge room and dozed for a while on the couch.

At seven a.m. Talya phoned Vanessa and told her the labour had started. When she hung up, she said Vanessa's children – ten year-old Rebecca and six year old Felix – were very excited. While Talya and I had breakfast, we talked about the way history was repeating itself. When I had my first child, Vanessa had been about the same age that Rebecca was now.

'Vanessa was eleven when I had Keir,' I said, 'and terribly excited. When Race rang from the hospital she answered the phone. He told her it was a boy and how much he weighed and then she rang all the relatives and passed on the news. She was a very proud messenger-girl.'

We talked about how much Vanessa and her older sister Jane had helped me when Keir and Talya were babies. Now Talya's nieces and nephews would be able to help her in turn. My three step-children, Sean forty-five, Jane forty-two, and Vanessa forty, were all married and each had a boy and a girl.

As we talked about the extended family, I reflected on its advantages. It had not always been easy, but one of the benefits was the close relationship that Keir and Talya had with their older brothers and sisters and their nieces and nephews. While we talked, Talya stopped whenever there was a contraction. She was bearing the pain well, sometimes standing up and sometimes leaning on a chair.

At nine a.m. Vanessa arrived, bright and cheerful. The contractions were still fluctuating and things were moving slowly. We sat in the kitchen chatting, mainly about childbirth. I described Keir's birth which was a straightforward labour, but I said little about Talya's birth. She knew that I haemorrhaged and nearly died, but this was not the time to go into details.

Instead, we discussed Vanessa's experience. 'With Rebecca,' she said, 'it was too long. She wasn't coming out and we waited and waited for the doctor. As soon as he arrived, he said he'd have to use the forceps to get her out. I found out later she had the cord around her neck too.' She turned to Talya: 'At least your doctor is just around the corner.' Talya was booked into a public hospital and was very happy with her obstetrician, Dr McCarthy, who was also her G.P.

We talked about the pain and whether breathing exercises helped. 'I don't think they take the pain away,' I said, 'but they give you something else to concentrate on.' Vanessa asked Talya if she wanted an epidural to block out the pain, but Talya said she would only have one if she couldn't cope naturally. As we talked, it felt very good to be taking part in an age-old ritual of women's business.

Vanessa and I asked Talya if she had chosen names for the baby. She had decided not to ask the sex of the baby when she had the ultra-sound, as she wanted it to be a surprise. We'd discussed names before, but now she'd finally made a decision. 'If it's a boy it will be Caleb Fabian, and if it's a girl it will be Ayesha,' she said. 'Caleb is an old biblical name and Ayesha is Arabic. The Fabian is for Dad of course.'

We smiled. Race's main occupation was running the Australian Fabian Society, a left-leaning think tank. It was based on the British Fabian Society founded by George Bernard Shaw and Sydney and Beatrice Webb. 'He'll be thrilled,' I said. 'You know that if I had twins he wanted to call them Sydney and Beatrice, after the Webbs.'

Talya made a face. 'I'm glad I wasn't a twin, then.' We laughed.

We talked about Javier and I asked if he was getting used to the idea of being a father. 'He's still coming to terms with it,' she said. 'I'll show him the baby as soon as it's born. I hope he'll want to have some involvement and maybe his parents too.' She stopped talking while a contraction gripped her and she leaned against the kitchen bench and breathed slowly.

At noon we had lunch. Vanessa had brought some smoked salmon sandwiches and fruit scones and we made tea and coffee. The contractions were now averaging about seven minutes apart. By one p.m. the contractions were five minutes apart and regular. At last it was time to go to the hospital, which was nearby.

We were shown into a large labour room with a hospital bed flanked by medical equipment. Annette, the midwife, was in the hospital uniform, a black and white shirt over black pants. She smiled at how many bags we were carrying, especially Vanessa's large camera bag. The room was warm and we took off our jumpers. Talya wore a large man's T-shirt and pyjama pants and tied her long hair back in a pony tail.

Vanessa started assembling the video camera and digital camera. Talya sat on a large rubber ball and Annette put a small machine against her belly to read the baby's heartbeat. It sounded very loud and fast, *chunka-chunka-chunk*, like a little train going along a track. It was even louder during a contraction. Then Annette strapped a belt and wires onto Talya's belly, connected to a foetal heart monitor. Talya was very calm and relaxed, making jokes between contractions. We had a five cents bet on when the baby would be born. I said six p.m., Vanessa said eight p.m. and Talya said nine p.m.

We looked at the typed notes from the ante-natal class about the different stages of childbirth. The early stage had a drawing of a smiling face, but in the active stage the mouth was in a straight line, no longer smiling. Later on, in transition stage, the mouth was very much turned down.

By two-thirty p.m. the contractions were getting stronger and Talya tried various positions to ease the pain, sometimes kneeling on the bed on all fours and sometimes leaning over a bean bag on the bed. Vanessa started massaging her lower back and I took over while Vanessa got a hot pack and held it where we had been massaging.

Annette brought in an aromatherapy burner and we put in some oils. Soon the room smelt faintly of eucalyptus and we heard the soothing strains of the hospital's relaxation CD. Talya was hot and flushed now and Vanessa put some peppermint oil on a wet cloth and sponged her face. I watched Talya and Vanessa and thought how lucky I was to be surrounded by such strong, capable women. I was tired after being awake since two a.m. and a bit anxious about what was to come. I was happy for Ness to take the lead about what we should do.

Talya took off her clothes and lay on her side, naked except for the hospital wristband. I noticed how natural she was and how different the birth procedure was to mine. I remembered a delivery room like an operating theatre, all bright lights, stainless steel and white walls. I had worn a hospital gown and lain on the bed throughout, with Race beside me. I thought of my mother's experience of childbirth. She always said that as soon as it became painful she grabbed an anaesthetic mask and put it over her face and remembered nothing afterwards.

Talya was lying on her back now with the sheet over her and her eyes shut. Her face was creased with pain. Then suddenly her waters broke and gushed all over the bed. This was a relief, as it meant things were progressing. Her obstetrician, Dr McCarthy, walked in as we stood around the bed. He was a good-looking man about forty, dressed casually in a shirt and white coat. 'That's good timing,' he said, 'I was just coming in to break the waters.' He chatted with Talya while the nurses cleaned her up and changed the sheets. Then he bent over to examine the cervix. He seemed not to notice Talya's nakedness.

'You're only five centimetres dilated,' he said. 'You need ten to be fully dilated so I need to stretch the cervix to encourage it.' As he did so Talya said, 'Christ,' a couple of times forcefully, and Vanessa and I smiled at each other, knowing that the doctor was Catholic.

'The cervix is still facing to the side, where it's been for weeks,' he said. 'This will right itself as labour progresses.' He then explained that if the labour continued for a long time with variable contractions – pushing the baby in and out instead of out – he would need to accelerate it. He left, saying that he would be in touch with progress on the phone and would come back in four hours if not before. Four hours! It was now about four p.m. and she'd been in labour fourteen hours. I gave Talya a hug and wished I could speed things up for her. She moved restlessly around the room.

Now that the waters had broken, the contractions were more painful. Annette said they were four minutes apart and she wanted them to get down to two minutes apart. Talya lay on the bed again. She was now silent during contractions and we could see from her face and body that she was in considerable pain. In between, Ness and I gave her sips of an energy drink and she nibbled on a fruit bar. I massaged her back and thought how brave she was, suffering silently just as I had done in my turn. She asked for another hot pack.

At five p.m. she went into 'transition' stage, where the contractions are very strong and close together. Talya groaned and said, 'The pain is getting worse.'

'I remember it,' I said. 'Race was reading to me from a book on natural childbirth and he said, "the contractions are like waves rolling in to the shore", and I said, "it's more like two bloody great iron pincers coming from both sides to grab you".'

Talya smiled weakly. Her face was tired and strained and there were grey shadows around her eyes. She had not slept the previous night and I was feeling dazed with tiredness myself. She was silent and brave with each contraction but suddenly said, 'Shoot me now,' and smiled weakly. Annette offered some laughing gas and Talya put on the mask, but after a few minutes ripped it off. 'It's not helping at all,' she said, 'It makes me feel nauseous and claustrophobic.' Annette recommended an injection of pethidine and Talya agreed. I watched with relief as Annette injected it into her arm, but about ten minutes later Talya said the pain was still as bad, and asked for an epidural.

Annette said gently, 'You need to give the pethidine more time to work, Talya. Dr McCarthy is coming at seven p.m. It's five-twenty now.'

'Oh God, I can't take too much of this,' Talya said.

Vanessa and I exchanged glances. We could see she was in a lot of pain and that the labour was taking a long time. An assistant midwife came in to help. I took her aside and asked quietly about the epidural. She said there were disadvantages to having one. 'Various pieces of equipment would be attached to Talya and it could slow down the labour,' she said. 'There's much more intervention that way.' I hoped Talya would not need it, but said nothing as she had to make the decision herself. Ness and I bathed her face with a damp cloth and massaged her back.

Talya was lying on her side now with the sheet over her. The contractions were quite close together. She kept her eyes closed and said the pethidine had not eased the pain. She was calmer however and Annette explained that the pethidine had the effect of distancing her from everything and focusing on the contractions. Annette kept telling Talya she was doing brilliantly, and Ness and I reassured her too and gave her drinks, massages and sponged her face.

At six p.m. Talya again asked for an epidural. Shortly afterwards Dr McCarthy arrived and examined her. He said the cervix was now eight to nine centimetres dilated and would soon be ten centimetres and that he preferred not to do an epidural because it would slow down the birth process. Talya said if she was nearly ten centimetres dilated then she would manage without it.

At seven p.m. Talya finally wanted to push. 'That's great news,' Dr McCarthy said and we all looked at each other with relief. Annette helped Talya sit up and she went red in the face as she pushed. At eight p.m. Dr McCarthy said she was now fully dilated, which made us all happy. Talya was sitting up now with her legs wide apart. She pushed again, going bright red in the face and neck and chest.

I put my hand on her shoulder and said, 'When I gave birth to Keir, Race said I went a beetroot colour and he thought I would burst. The midwife asked me to slow down, but it was like a steam-train; there was no way I could do that.' Talya nodded and at the next push she did a breathing exercise, inhaling deeply and exhaling with short puffs.

When the contraction was over, Annette put the monitor on Talya's belly and we heard the baby's heart loudly with its rapid *chunka-chunka–chunk* sound. Talya's eyes were closed and her face was clenched with pain.

I wiped her face with a cool cloth and then moved down the bed to see what was happening. We waited for the next contraction and then Annette showed us the baby's head. It was about the size of a twenty-cent piece. Vanessa filmed it with the video camera.

Half an hour later, Talya tried a different position. We placed the beanbag on the bed and she leaned over it as she pushed. Ness took a photo. Annette smiled and said, 'Childbirth is not very elegant, is it!' By nine p.m. Talya was on her back again, letting out a big sigh with each push, red in the face. The baby's head came out a little, but then went back in again. Talya was pushing valiantly but becoming exhausted. She had now been in labour nineteen hours.

I felt worried because her contractions seemed to be slowing down, but I said nothing. Dr McCarthy then explained that the baby was on its side trying to turn the corner to come out, but not succeeding. He said he was going to help things along by using a suction cap on the baby's head and an episiotomy. I remembered having an episiotomy with both my children and was glad because it would enlarge the space for the baby to come out.

The nurses brought a small operating table to the bed with the instruments lined up and put Talya's legs in stirrups. Dr McCarthy swabbed between the legs with antiseptic and gave her a local anaesthetic. He then made a large incision between the vagina and the back passage. Blood ran everywhere. I turned away.

When I looked again Dr McCarthy was attaching a suction cap to the baby's head. He waited for the next contraction and then pulled gently on the cord attached to the cap. Blood oozed out from the cut. The baby's head emerged fully and then stopped, like a cork in a bottle. 'It's head is out,' I said to Talya excitedly, 'it's got dark hair.' The baby was covered in blood and its eyes were closed tight. Then it made a little cry and started breathing. Dr McCarthy removed the suction cap and wiped some of the blood away.

He then moved aside and looked at Vanessa, who was holding the camera, and said politely, 'Are you getting everything?' We laughed and she moved closer in. Talya sat up and touched the baby's head and said, 'I'm worried it can't breathe properly. Can I push?'

'No, we need the force of the contraction.' Dr McCarthy held the baby's head gently and with the next contraction he lifted out the arms, which were like little pink sausages. Then the stomach emerged with the dark red umbilical cord attached. Vanessa kept filming and we told Talya what was happening.

Soon Dr McCarthy had the legs out and he laid the baby on Talya's stomach. Annette covered it with a white towel and wiped some more blood off its head. I rushed around the bed to look and Talya said, 'It's a boy! It's Caleb Fabian!' She gazed at him in wonder. Ness and I congratulated her and I felt as excited as though I'd given birth myself. I looked at my watch, it was nine forty-five p.m. She'd been in labour for twenty hours. I kissed her and felt close to tears. At last it was over and she and the baby were all right.

Dr McCarthy clamped the cord and cut it. The nurse wrapped the baby in the towel and gave him to Talya who smiled radiantly and kissed his head. He made little noises and Talya stroked him and said, 'He's gorgeous.' Annette opened the towel a little so we could see more of him. His head was no longer squashed and he seemed a pretty baby, without blemishes. He opened and shut his eyes slowly and showed his little pink tongue. His tiny fingers fanned out. 'He's beautiful,' we said as Annette covered him up again.

While Talya held him, I picked up the phone by the bed and called Race. He was with Sean and Sean's son Hagan. I told Race it was a boy and that his name was Caleb Fabian. Race was delighted with this and very relieved that Talya and the baby were all right. I put Talya on the phone and she said, 'I'm exhausted Dad, but elated. For the last few hours I thought I couldn't go on any longer, but now I'm all right.'

While she was on the phone the baby started quivering and Annette said, 'He's cold, we'd better weigh him.' She took him to the scales and removed his towel and laid him down under a heat lamp, naked and grizzling. She told us he was 8 lb 2½ ounces or 3.75 kg. We congratulated her on having such a big healthy baby and said it was strange, because the ultrasound in recent weeks had suggested the baby was underweight. We could see him clearly now and he looked lovely. His little body was soft and rounded. Talya was still on the phone to Race and asked him to come in to the hospital with Sean and Hagan.

Dr McCarthy said, 'I'd better examine him,' and placed him on a towel near the scales. Ness and I watched while he looked in the baby's eyes, ears and mouth and then felt his heart and pressed his abdomen, checking all his tiny organs. He took each leg and gently rotated it to check the hips. Caleb protested with a few grizzles. When Dr McCarthy had finished, Annette swaddled the baby in another towel and a bunny rug and gave him back to Talya. Vanessa picked up the phone to call her family.

It was now time to deliver the afterbirth. Dr McCarthy injected Talya with some oxytocin and massaged the uterus. The placenta came out with a gush of blood. It looked like a large and bloody football and he put it in a bowl and showed us. It had kept the baby alive for nine months.

Talya was now bleeding a lot and I was worried, remembering how I'd haemorrhaged after her birth. Dr McCarthy gave her an injection to stop the bleeding. Then he told her he was going to do the stitches. He swabbed her between the legs with antiseptic and started stitching with a long, strong thread. He seemed to be stitching for nearly an hour. Towards the end I asked how many stitches there were and he said diplomatically, 'One continuous stitch.' The assistant midwife turned to me and smiled and said, 'He asked for another packet of thread, so that means there are a lot.' When he'd finished, Talya lay back under the sheet and we gave her another drink and a snack.

At eleven p.m. Race arrived with Sean and Hagan and they took turns holding Caleb. Race was first and stared at the baby, fascinated, while the rest of us looked on. We all had huge grins. 'He's a handsome little fellow, isn't he,' said Ness. Sean then held him and was so excited that fourteen-year-old Hagan said, 'I want you and Mum to have another baby.' Sean laughed and said, 'It's a bit late now.'

Annette put Caleb on Talya's breast and we watched him have a little suck and then fall asleep. The nurse said that soon they would take Talya upstairs to her room and give her a shower and some food. They would bath the baby and then Talya would be left to sleep. As we said goodbye, I remembered the bet about when the baby would be born and said, 'You win, Talya. You said nine p.m. and that was the closest. It was nearly ten p.m. when he was born.' She smiled.

As Race and I walked to the car he said, 'How do you feel?'

'Wrecked,' I said, 'physically and emotionally. But it was one of the greatest events of my life.'

Two days after the birth Talya contacted Javier and he came into the hospital and saw his son for the first time. Afterwards she told us he stayed for two hours and when it was time to leave he didn't want to go. Talya took a photo of him holding Caleb and kissing him. Javier told Talya he would like to teach Caleb Spanish, his first language, and she said she would love Caleb to be bilingual. Javier apologised for his confusion when he first heard she was pregnant and thanked her for her patience. When she relayed all this to Race and me I felt overjoyed. It looked like Caleb would have two parents who loved him, and maybe two sets of grandparents. He was a lucky baby.

10

Caleb's first month

'Somehow the world I was in now, helping to care for a new baby, seemed more real than the one I saw out there and read about in the newspaper each morning.'

Three days after the birth, I took Talya home from the hospital. Now at last I could help with my new grandson. I'd forgotten how wonderful it was to hold a new-born baby. Having a grandchild allows you to experience it all over again, without the anxiety and responsibility. It's pure pleasure. Caleb was so small that he could lie in the crook of my arm. He had fine, straight, brown hair, large blue eyes that looked around alertly, soft pink skin and a rosebud mouth.

We found him endlessly fascinating to watch. When he slept in his pram or baby capsule, his little mouth pursed and quivered, perhaps dreaming of his mother's milk. His eyelids flickered, he frowned slightly and different expressions flitted across his face. Sometimes he was in pain and his legs pulled up and he made a cry. Sometimes his hands opened out like baby starfish and flung outwards, which startled him. I took hold of his hands to calm him, marvelling at the tiny bones. His fingers curled around mine and gripped tightly.

When he became restless, I scooped him up and held him against my chest, with his head under my chin. Then I sat back and felt his warmth. His head was soft and his heart beat rapidly. He liked that position, feeling my own heartbeat and warmth in response. I was filled with the same rush of love and protectiveness I had when my children were small. I would have thrown myself under a train to save them, and now I felt the same way about him.

I looked up and smiled at Talya, who was watching. She smiled back. Having this child had brought us close together. We saw each other nearly every day now or talked on the phone. It was the age-old mother-daughter bond, the shared experience. Much passed between us in looks and smiles, without words. She was transformed by motherhood, happy and contented, in love with her baby and so competent in handling him.

I thought back to the Talya of a year earlier, and asked if she missed the party girl who drank and smoked and stayed up all night. She laughed and said, 'Not at all. I was getting really bored with her and looking for something else to focus on.' She looked at Caleb adoringly and said, 'Sometimes I can't believe all this is real. He's so perfect. I'm not sure I deserve it.'

'Of course you do.'

I was so proud of her, with her newfound happiness and maturity. She had not followed the 'normal' path of school, university, career, marriage and children. She had done things differently, and maybe always would. I did the same, but in a more cautious way. We had both left

Australia in our twenties, lived overseas, took risks, had adventures and found our focus when we returned home at the age of twenty-six. She had faced tough challenges, and met them each time.

I knew so little about her life in Japan, but I hoped one day she would write about it, using her diaries. It was a colourful story. She now planned to return to study, then to work and one day to write. But all that was in the future. For the moment, motherhood was all absorbing, along with rebuilding her life in Melbourne with her family and friends.

Caleb started to be restless and she showed me how to change his nappy, in case I'd forgotten after so many years. We went into the nursery, filled with autumn sunlight. She showed me how to fold a nappy in a kite shape with the thickest part in the middle. I placed Caleb on the changing-table and removed the bunny rug which swaddled him. He was waiting for a feed and moved his mouth and made little noises. Talya stood by in case I needed help.

I was impressed by how well she was handling her parents – not telling us what to do, but letting us learn by practising. I undid his jumpsuit and took out his legs. He didn't like the cold and grizzled. Then it became complicated – taking off the wet plastic 'snib' covering the nappy, washing and drying his naked bottom and smearing it with cream while he wriggled and kicked, putting on a clean nappy and snib and then putting him back into the jumpsuit. His cries became louder and louder and I felt like I was in the four minute mile.

Finally I swaddled him in a clean blanket and picked

him up. He calmed a little and I gave him to Talya who was sitting in the rocking chair ready to feed. He started sucking immediately, his little hand on her breast, his chin working up and down. He was at peace again, and we felt the tension disappear. Talya and I smiled at each other. The race was over until the next time.

While I watched, I remembered how exhausting it was in the first few weeks home with a new baby. Race and I had discussed this before Caleb's birth and he had agreed to share the grand-parenting role. Talya had stitches and it hurt her to walk and she was feeding Caleb every two to three hours. Race and I decided that for the first two weeks we would do shifts. He would help during the night and I would go during the day.

So on her first night home, Race slept on the couch in her lounge-room with Caleb in the pram beside him. When Caleb woke, Race changed his nappy and took him to Talya who fed him in her warm bed, then put him back to sleep in the pram. After breakfast, Race came home and told me about his shift. He sat on the end of our bed where I was reading the newspaper, and he tried to remember the sequence of events.

'Let's see now, he was restless about eleven p.m. and Talya went to sleep in her room. I rocked him in my arms for an hour or so until he settled down, but when I put him in the pram he woke up again and cried. I tried pushing the pram up and down but it didn't help much. I ended up lying on the couch with him asleep on my chest until he woke for the next feed. After that he slept in the pram all night, apart from waking up for feeds. She was feeding him when I left.'

I was intensely interested in all this. 'You lay with him on your chest!' I said. 'Weren't you falling asleep?'

He rubbed his eyes and yawned. 'Yes, I think I slept too. It's all a bit of a blur.'

We smiled at each other and talked about our plans for the day. He worked from home and I was going to Talya's for the day and then on to see my mother. There was no time now to think of my writing – that would have to come later. This baby was a new project for Race and me, a late-in-life shared love object. Race was doing what he'd missed out on with his own five children, helping to care for a newborn child. Now, a white haired man of sixty-seven, he was enjoying his grandchildren. Like most men, he did not show his emotions very much, but I could already see his love for this new baby. In the hospital, I'd watched him pick up Caleb and give him little kisses on the head, like a bird pecking at a seed.

I dressed hurriedly and went to Talya's. I told her to catch up on some sleep while I took Caleb to a park nearby. I set out with the pram along the footpath, which was very uneven. Caleb wore a little woollen hat and was tucked in warmly with extra blankets. He slept lightly, his head turned to one side, but with each bump of the pram he twitched. It was my first chance to explore the neighbourhood on foot.

Talya had rented a flat in East Brighton, not far from where I grew up. East Brighton used to be the poor cousin, but now it was trying hard to catch up to affluent Brighton which was nearer the sea. East Brighton was an area of family homes, forty or fifty years old. Some were still in their original state, with rusty roofs and peeling paint, but most had been renovated and expanded, with another storey on top or an extension out the back.

The streets were quiet and there were no people about, except for workmen. A van outside one house said, 'Jim's Mowing' and two 'Jims' were busy in the garden. Another van advertised floor sanding and the noise of the machine grated through the window. I turned a corner and saw a young mother approaching with a small child in a pusher, putting advertising material in letterboxes. She smiled and said hello. I stopped walking and she looked into the pram.

'Oh, he's so tiny, how old is he?' She turned to her child and said, 'Look at the little baby, Emma.'

'He's only four days old,' I said. 'I'm his grandmother. My daughter's asleep.'

'Oh, he's beautiful. You forget how small they are. Where does your daughter live?'

'In the next street.' I waved in that direction.

'I walk around here twice a week, delivering these.' She gestured at the brochures. 'I figure, I need to get out and walk anyway, so why not do this at the same time?'

'It's a great idea.'

We said goodbye and moved off. I liked this camaraderie of women with small children. This was a family place, and I hoped it would be easy for Talya to meet other young mothers in the neighbourhood. I walked up and down the side streets, getting to know the area. We came to a large fence which shielded the neighbourhood from a highway. Through a gap in the fence I saw six lanes of cars streaming past and heard the noise. I turned back into the quiet street. Somewhere out there was the 'real' world, but I preferred this peaceful enclave.

I thought about the meaning of the 'real' world. Somehow the world I was in now, helping to care for a new baby, seemed more real than the one I saw out there and read about in the newspaper each morning. Once my life had been at high speed too, meeting 'important' people and jumping on and off planes. I wasn't missing it for a minute.

Caleb was restless now, wriggling around in the pram and grizzling. I stopped walking and patted him until he was calm and lay him down again. We soon reached the park, which was a small grassy space with trees around the edge. It had two swings, a red climbing frame and a small shelter shed. I'd been walking for nearly an hour and was glad to sit down.

I got out my newspaper, but Caleb was grizzling again. He had wind and pulled his little legs up in pain. I picked him up and cuddled him. He wouldn't settle, so I took him to the swings and sat down gingerly on one, with him against my chest. I found a way of holding him and the swing at the same time, and gently rocked back and forth. He stopped crying. I swung a bit higher, holding him tightly. He loved it. His head was soft and warm and smelled so sweet. I felt a sense of triumph and happiness. What could be nicer than this? I stayed on the swing until he started whimpering again. Soon it would be time for his next feed. I put him back in the pram and turned for home.

While Talya fed him, I helped with the housework. That evening, Race arrived and the three of us sat by the heater in the lounge-room. We ate dinner, watched the news on television and took it in turns to cuddle Caleb. I felt blessed. In one of life's unexpected twists, we were having the family life I'd always wanted but never had when my children were small, because politics kept Race away from home, or preoccupied when he was there.

Three weeks later, I sat in Talya's light-filled kitchen, while Caleb slept in his cot in the nursery. It was three in the afternoon and across the hall, Talya slept in her room. It was early June. Winter had arrived, and as I sat in the warm, silent flat, I looked out on a grey sky where the trees tossed from side to side. Race was now in the United States on a lecture tour and Talya was alone at night with Caleb. He still fed every three hours and was often awake at night. She was struggling to get enough sleep, just as I did with her, twenty-six years earlier.

We discussed the sleep problem daily. Talya read all the baby books, consulted with friends and her older siblings and visited the Maternal and Child Health Centre to get advice. Much of it was contradictory. We watched a video on how to settle a crying baby. A kindly, plump mothercraft nurse came on the screen and told us that with her technique we could fix a baby or toddler's sleeping problems within an hour. Her method was called 'controlled comforting.' It sounded suspiciously like a more brutal method called 'controlled crying.'

The mothercraft nurse stood by a cot, holding a small baby. She told us that babies adapt to a ritual, and need to get used to sleeping in their cot and not being picked up every time they cry. 'If you pick them up and get them to sleep in your arms,' she said, 'and then put them down in their cot, they'll wake later and be distressed because they're not in your arms.' She said her method was to teach them to get themselves to sleep.

She took the baby and swaddled him in a blanket, and put him in the cot. She turned him on his side and patted him gently while he grizzled. The grizzles got louder and she raised her voice and spoke to the camera. 'After a while, Bubby will stop crying and go to sleep,' she said. 'If he's still crying after fifteen minutes, you can pick him up and cuddle him a bit to comfort him, and then put him back in the cot and repeat the patting process. You keep this up until he falls asleep. When he's asleep you turn him on his back.'

The camera cut to the baby asleep on his side. The mothercraft nurse beamed and turned him on his back where he continued to sleep. She smiled at us triumphantly. 'After a while he'll learn to put himself to sleep in the cot,' she said. 'If he wakes later, he'll know how to put himself back to sleep. If you want to have a dummy, it's up to you, but if you have a dummy and he wakes up, he'll need the dummy in order to get to sleep again.'

Talya and I were impressed. It all sounded so simple and logical. 'I wish I'd had that video when you were a baby,' I said. 'I had months of sleepless nights, it was really terrible.'

'Sorry Mum.'

I laughed. 'It wasn't your fault. It was probably because there were a lot of other problems in my life at that time.'

Talya decided to try the method straight away. At nine p.m. after his feed, when he was tired and grizzling, she put him down in his cot without his dummy and rocked him in the approved manner. He did not settle. After fifteen minutes she picked him up and repeated the process. After a while he calmed down and she joined me in the lounge room. A loud cry came down the hallway and she returned to the nursery. About an hour later, he appeared to be sleeping, so I wished her well and went home.

I woke at six-thirty a.m. and wondered how she was managing. The phone rang at seven a.m. 'He was awake from when you left, right up until 5 o'clock this morning,' she said in a little voice.

'Oh no! You poor thing! What happened? What's he doing now?'

'He's feeding now. I tried that patting business all night, but the most he ever slept was twenty minutes at a time and then he woke up again and cried. At three a.m. I thought, stuff this; I'm giving him the bloody dummy. That helped a bit, but he didn't sleep properly until five a.m. Then we both slept for a couple of hours until he woke for his next feed.'

'You must feel terrible. I'll come over as soon as I've had a shower.'

'I'm all right,' she said, but sounded exhausted.

'I think you need to consult an expert about it. Phone the Maternal and Child Health Centre nurse and talk to her again.'

When I arrived, Caleb was sleeping, and he remained peaceful all day. He was now a model baby, sleeping, feeding and having lovely wakeful periods when he gazed around alertly. We gave him a bath and he gurgled with delight, kicking and splashing wildly. Later in the day Talya went into the bedroom and phoned the nurse at the Maternal and Child Health Centre. She emerged, beaming.

'She said not to worry about the video; he's too young for that method. It works for some babies and not for others. She said if he doesn't settle after a while, just pick him up and cuddle him or do whatever it takes to calm him down. She says some babies don't settle properly at night until three months. There are no simple solutions. You just have to do what you can to get through this period.'

'That's eight weeks more,' I wailed.

She laughed. 'Yes, but it's a relief not to have to do that bloody patting again. I felt like such a cruel mother last night.'

We sat and played with him and talked quietly about some other tips she had been given by the Maternal and Child Health Centre nurse. Talya had started to recognise now when he was getting tired, and was putting him to sleep as soon as he yawned or fussed, instead of leaving it a bit longer. It seemed that he could easily become over-tired, and then could not calm himself. For the rest of the day he was angelic. I held him in my arms and kissed his forehead. He smelled sweet and slightly milky. I propped him on my knees and held his little hands and watched his face while he looked around. I sang to him and he looked at me, listening.

One of the small miracles wrought by this tiny baby was the change in Javier, Caleb's father. Since Caleb's birth he'd phoned Talya every night and had seen Caleb as often as he could. He wanted to help financially and in other ways as well.

I was immensely pleased by this development and by the way Talya and Javier were handling this 'post-modern' relationship. He was single and lived in a flat on the other side of town. They were not in love, but they seemed to be good friends. When Caleb was two weeks old, Talya made a video of Javier playing with Caleb, which she showed me. I liked Javier's dry sense of humour and the way he played gently with Caleb.

When Caleb was four weeks old, Talya organised a family party at our place, and Javier agreed to come. We were impressed that he was brave enough to meet our large family all at once – Race and me and Talya's brothers and sisters, their partners and children. He arrived with gifts and charmed us all. I could see that he was shy underneath and very polite. Talya had told me he was an artist, preparing an exhibition, and worked in a variety of jobs to make money. He was tall and slim and very good looking, with olive skin, dark eyes and black hair.

When everyone had gone, Javier went upstairs with Talya to bath Caleb. I cleaned up the house, smiling to myself as I heard the murmur of their voices upstairs and laughter and splashing. When I went upstairs later, Javier was learning to change a nappy, with Talya looking on proudly. He looked up and grinned. When it was time for him to leave, he thanked me and said he was surprised that he was not 'grilled' more by the family.

'We wouldn't do that,' I smiled. 'We wanted you to feel welcome.'

His face softened. 'I did. Thank you for that.'

A week later, he took Talya to meet his parents. She told me about it on the phone the next morning. 'His parents are very nice and friendly. His dad was watching the football on the TV, but he played with Caleb on his knee.'

'What about the mother?'

'She held Caleb for a little while, then the dad wanted him and she gave him back. Javier gave Caleb a bath and his mother stood by nervously with a towel. His dad looked in from time to time and then went back to the footy.'

I loved this story, and asked: 'Was Javier trying to impress his mother by bathing the baby?'

'Yes, and he told her he'd changed about forty nappies, and I said to her, "that's a bit of an exaggeration," and she rolled her eyes and said, "Javier he always talks too much." She kept saying to me, "I didn't believe it when Javier told me about the baby, I didn't believe it."'

'Did you meet his brother?'

'Yes, his younger brother, who was painting the house. He was nice. His other brother lives in Tasmania.'

'Did they give you something to eat?'

'His mother kept asking if I'd stay for a meal, but I was worried that Caleb was going to start grizzling, so I didn't stay.'

We talked some more about the family. She told me that Javier didn't want domesticity and she couldn't make her life with him. She hoped in a few years time to marry someone and have more children. I said I was impressed though by how well she and Javier were getting on and how good he was with Caleb.

'We've always got on well,' she said. 'We used to talk about that. His parents are like you and Dad, you discuss things rationally and you don't fight. Javier and I are the same. He says I can live at his place and not pay rent, but I don't want that. I like my independence.'

That night, Javier stayed at her place for the first time, in case she had a wakeful night with Caleb. The next morning she told me Javier didn't sleep at all, but sat reading in the lounge room, and got up to change the nappy and put Caleb back in his cot after each feed.

'Was that helpful? Will you have him stay again?'

'Maybe, but Javier wants to play with Caleb in the middle of the night instead of putting him back to sleep. I don't want Caleb to get the idea you can have playtime in the middle of the night.' We laughed. During the day Talya liked the way Javier played with Caleb. Javier, like most fathers, played very actively and talked a lot to the baby. He made jokes and pretended to have conversations with him. He told Caleb he would teach him to play the guitar and play footy, and teach him Spanish.

I was filled with happiness at all this. Everything was working out well for Talya and Caleb. Now that he was four weeks old I no longer needed to go every day. I could start to think about other things. I was keen to get back to my writing, but there was another baby who was demanding my attention – my ninety-five year old mother.

11

Mum and Caleb

'Where had my lovely mother gone, the one who was always happy and smiling?'

My mother did not like sharing me. After Caleb's birth, she became like a two-year-old who plays up in order to get attention when their mother has a new baby. I'd noticed the previous year, when she was in and out of hospital, that she was becoming in some ways like a small child again, dependent, weak and afraid. Now her fears about her health and age were overlaid by fears that I was not as attentive as before. She, who was always so strong and independent and cheerful, had become depressed and difficult and demanding.

Two days after Caleb's birth, I took her into the hospital and we posed for a 'four generations' photograph. Mum was dressed up in her best blue suit and matching silk blouse, but she didn't smile. We took a photo of her holding Caleb, and we congratulated her on being a great-grandmother, but she still didn't smile.

A few days later I went to my mother's room and gave her the photograph of her and Caleb. She looked at it and quickly put it in a drawer. Normally she displayed photos on the desk by her bed.

'Aren't you going to show the photo to your friends?' I asked.

She sat down on the bed and looked embarrassed. 'How can I tell them about it? They'll say, "I didn't know your granddaughter was married. Who did she marry?"'

This had been on her mind for months. I sat down beside her and took her hand. She was tiny now, less than five feet tall, white haired and shrunken. Her face was pale and strained and her usual smiles were gone.

'We've discussed this,' I said. 'They may not ask if she's married, but if they do, just tell the truth. She's friends with the father of the baby, but they're not married.'

Her eyes flashed. 'I couldn't possibly say that. You don't understand what they're like. One lady here has twenty-three grandchildren and they all got married in church. They all became schoolteachers or professional people.'

I smiled at this. 'They just hide their problems, Mum. Lots of people nowadays live together without getting married. I'll bet the people here have all got something unusual in their families. They just don't talk about it.'

'There's only one person here I can tell. That's Joan Woodford.' She lowered her voice. 'Her daughter married an Indian.'

I laughed. 'What's wrong with that?'

'You don't understand, dear. This is another generation. They're set in their ways; they're very conservative you know.'

Yes, I did know. In her genteel retirement home the old ladies dressed in high heels and jewellery just to totter to the dining room with their walking frames. They all voted conservatively and when Australia flirted with the Republican vote, they declared themselves to be strongly in favour of retaining the monarchy.

I was keeping up my visits to my mother as well as going to Talya's house each day, but it was not enough. While I was at Talya's one day, my mother phoned. Her voice was croaky and frightened.

'I'm not at all well, not at all,' she said. 'I've got a sore eye and I think it might be infected. It feels like there's something in it.'

It was an hour's drive from Talya's to Mum's, but I went over that afternoon and got some eye drops from the chemist.

The next day she phoned again. 'I need you desperately. You know they changed our phone numbers here. Well, they asked us to tell people that we have a new phone number. I went through the old address book Dad and I had, and most of the people in it are dead. I don't know how to notify the rest of them. You'll have to come round and do it for me.'

I went around the next day and asked her to tell me who she wanted to notify. We went through the address book, skipping past the names she'd crossed out. 'What about Mrs B__?' I asked.

'Oh no, I never want to see her again.'

'But you and Dad were close friends with them.'

'That was just because your father was keen on her. I never liked her. Cross her out.'

I turned over a page. 'What about Dad's colleague, R___?'

'Blind and deaf, cross him out.'

We continued in this manner until we had a small list of about twenty people, mostly younger relatives. That evening I sent out the letters. Two days later, I took her to the dentist. She moved so slowly that the outing took up half a day and then she wanted me to buy her lunch.

The following morning at breakfast she phoned again, with a suffering voice. I knew this voice well from my childhood. Normally she was cheerful and strong in those days – the beacon which lit up the family. But she was no good when she became ill. Even with a light cold, she'd take to her bed and get my father to wait on her, while she spoke to us all in that voice of death. We children used to roll our eyes at each other until she recovered and life went back to normal.

'My eye is still playing up,' she croaked. 'Can you take me to the eye doctor today please?'

I felt a surge of anger and said, 'For God's sake Mum, I can't just drop everything when you need me. I spent half a day with you yesterday. I'm really busy helping Talya at present. Can't you remember what it was like with a new baby? Can we do it later in the week? Talya really needs me at the moment.'

Silence. Then a small voice said, 'I need you too.'

'Why don't you take a taxi to your eye doctor? It's only a short distance, and the taxi can park at the back, next to the ramp for you to walk up. When you've finished, ask the receptionist to call you a taxi.'

There was a long silence. I felt guilty. She couldn't believe I was not coming. I said goodbye, and hurried off to Talya's place.

The next night I went to a political lecture with Race. At midnight, when I was in a deep sleep, the phone rang.

'Hello,' she croaked. 'I'm in a terrible state. I went to the eye doctor like you said and he gave me two medicines, and I can't read the instructions to put them in my eye.'

'Mum, it's *midnight*,' I said. 'Have you called the night staff? Can't they help you?'

'Oh, they're no use.'

'They are there to help you, have you called them?'

'One of them has gone to make me a cup of tea, because I'm so upset. They told me to go to sleep, but I can't. I'm in a terrible state. You can't imagine what it's like to be here and have bad eyes.' She started to cry. 'I don't want to go blind.'

'Mum, you're not going blind. What did the eye doctor say?'

'I went in the taxi and it was terrible. I dropped my bank card on the floor of the taxi when I had to pay him and I couldn't find it. When I got home I was just shaking all over. I can't take taxis any more, dear. I know you're busy, but you're all I've got. You're my rock, I feel like I've lost my right arm.'

I groaned inwardly and said, 'What did the eye doctor say?'

'He said I have an eye infection and I have to put some drops in, and I have to wash the eyelashes with some other stuff and I can't read the labels and I can't do it, it's all too complicated. I just can't cope.'

I told her I was going to phone the night staff and make sure they helped her, and that I would see her in the morning, and I hung up. I tried to sleep, but I had bad dreams for the rest of the night.

The next day I spoke to Eleanor, the manager of the retirement home and Janet, her deputy. 'We're looking after her eye drops,' Eleanor said. 'We're very sorry she phoned you at midnight. We would have stopped her if we'd known.'

I explained that she was upset because I was busy helping my daughter.

'You're squeezed in the middle, aren't you?' said Eleanor. 'I am too. My daughter has just had a miscarriage and lives in Queensland. I went up to see her and then my husband and my elderly mother started playing up because I wasn't spending enough time with them.'

Janet chipped in. 'My mother lives in Castlemaine, it's a two hour drive and I have to go every weekend and spend the day with her. Last year my daughter gave birth early, the day before my other daughter had her wedding. I was running from one to the other and my mother carried on like a pork chop.'

We laughed conspiratorially. 'All the old ladies here give their daughters a hard time,' said Eleanor. 'They don't do it to their sons.'

The following week, my mother complained about her eyes continually. I took her back to her eye doctor. He told her she had the beginnings of macular degeneration but her eyes were fine for her age. The infection was clearing up and she was not going blind. He said she could read everything except the telephone book.

'But I know they're not fine,' she said, shakily. 'They get blurry, and they get tired after I read for a while. Why have I got this infection?'

'Because you're old,' he said. 'Your eyes are deteriorating, but you're not going blind.'

I was delighted at his straight talking. No one had ever told her she was old before. Apart from her periods in hospital, she had been one of the fittest women in the retirement home, and her self-image was that of a woman much younger than her years. Maybe it was time she accepted that a ninety-five year old body has its limitations and they can't all be fixed.

'He doesn't know what he's talking about,' she said crossly when we got in the car. 'I know there's something wrong with my eyes. I was playing cards the other day and I had to stop because the cards on the table were blurry. I think we should get another opinion.'

Things got worse. She phoned me every few days to complain about her eyes or some other part of her body. One day it was a sore leg, another day it was a stomach pain. She kept telling me that she'd 'lost me' and was afraid. I contacted my brother, who was living in Spain and my sister, who lived interstate, and discussed the problem. They were very supportive, and agreed to phone her twice a week.

Andrée, an old family friend rang me. 'Your mother asked me to come over to see her,' she said, 'and then cried for about two hours. We had a big Confessional.'

'What about?'

'She's afraid that she's lost you because you're with the baby so much, but she also feels guilty because she has not been very positive about the baby. She's guilty that she hasn't told anyone in the retirement home about it. I've talked her into showing the photo to her friends as a first step.'

A couple of days later my mother phoned me with a

tearful voice. 'I need to see you urgently. I know there's a rift between us and I want to heal it. You're all I've got and I love you so much. I'm so depressed.'

I felt like shaking her, but I assured her there was no rift between us. 'I phone you or see you every few days, just as much as before, don't I?'

'It's not that. Your attitude has changed,' she croaked. 'You don't realise how sick I am. You think I'm making it all up. I'm terribly worried about my eyes. I want to see another eye doctor, I want a second opinion.'

I felt a potent mixture of anger, pity and guilt. She'd been to her own eye doctor twice, why should I take her to another bloody doctor? But I said nothing, and took her to my own eye doctor. He examined her and said because of the macular degeneration, her eyes would deteriorate later, but at the moment they were fine, and she was not going blind.

When we got outside, I held her arm as usual and said cheerfully, 'Well, that was good news, you're not going blind.'

She set her face stubbornly. 'I didn't say I was going blind.'

I glared at her. 'Yes you did. You said you were afraid you were going blind.'

'Oh no, I only said there might have been a slight *possibility*, that's all. Anyway, he said they will definitely get worse.'

We walked for a while in silence. Then, to change the subject, I spoke about Talya and the baby, and told her that he was now five weeks old, but he was still waking up through the night.

'Well, that's because you all pick him up too much during the day and you're spoiling him,' she said. I opened my mouth to say angrily, 'What rubbish!' but saw the jealousy, and said nothing.

Talya tried to help by suggesting that she bring the baby over to the retirement home, to show him off. But Mum was afraid of this and guilty, and became more depressed and difficult. I discussed this with Talya and I said, 'Just shoot me before I get like that,' but we both knew there was no way out. Old age was outside our control.

One night Race and I had friends to dinner and as I was standing in the kitchen pouring soup into bowls, I thought of my mother in her better days. It was she who taught me how to make a home into a warm, welcoming place. It was she who, on cold winter nights, sat us by the fire and brought us hot soup and crusty bread, delicious stews and puddings. I felt a rush of love for her again. She was fairly cheerful until Caleb arrived. Would I end up like her? And if I did, wouldn't I want people to be kind to me?

I confided in a friend who cared for a difficult mother for years until she died. 'You must defend your limits,' she said. 'No matter how much time you give them, it doesn't fix their problem.' That was just what I wanted to hear. I resolved to give my mother sympathy, but to limit my visits to twice a week, no matter how much she tried to manipulate me. My friend told me about a mutual friend who used to take her elderly mother out in a wheelchair. Every now and then she would let go of the wheelchair on a slope, and let it roll for a while before she grabbed hold of it again. We laughed.

The following Monday, my mother phoned. 'I know you all think I should have the baby over here to show people,' she said, 'so I've decided you can bring Talya and the baby on Friday.'

'That's great, Mum, but you don't need me. Talya could come by herself.'

'Oh no, I need you to hold my hand.'

The night before the visit, she phoned in a panic. 'You'll have to come over straight away. My blood pressure is very high. They've had to take it three times today.'

I was getting dressed to go out. I told her I couldn't come, and would see her the next day. 'Mum, you're just worried about the visit. You'll feel better when it's over.'

'People think I don't love this baby,' she said tearfully. 'I want to make amends, I've mucked things up.'

When we arrived at the retirement home on the Friday, my mother was smiling bravely. She showed us into the lounge room where a bunch of old ladies were sitting in chairs, waiting. Some of them were asleep. Talya was dressed up and set out to be charming to everyone, while my mother hovered in the doorway. Talya sat down beside a white haired lady with a large hearing aid, and showed her Caleb, asleep in her arms.

My mother approached and said, 'This is Mrs D__. She's a hundred years old.'

Mrs D__ looked at Caleb and shouted, 'How old is he?'

'Six weeks,' Talya said loudly.

'Ten weeks, fancy that,' said Mrs D.

Eleanor, the manager, came in and took Caleb in her

arms. 'He's lovely,' she said. 'It's so nice of you to bring him in to show us.'

An old lady holding a walking stick looked at Talya and said loudly, 'Where's the father?'

Talya paused and said, 'He's in Brunswick.'

Eleanor said quickly, 'He's at work, like all fathers.' My mother moved us out of the lounge-room and down the hall to meet her special friends. One of them gave Caleb a small poodle made of wool. They were friendly and kind.

The next morning I phoned my mother. 'The visit was a big success, wasn't it?' I said. 'You must be feeling very relieved.'

She sniffed. 'Tomorrow they'll be making a fuss of someone else's baby,' was all she would say. She told me she had not slept well because of 'restless legs' and was worried about having lost weight. She wanted me to take her to the doctor. When I took her later in the week, she told the doctor that she was depressed and thought she was 'cracking up.' He gave her a general check-up and said she was not sick, but as she was feeling down, he would give her some anti-depressants.

'Give *her* the prescription,' said my mother in a weak voice, waving a hand weakly in my direction, 'I'm too unwell to take care of anything any more.' The doctor handed me the prescription with a twinkle in his eye.

Driving her home after the doctor, she pulled down the sun visor and held her handbag over her eyes, saying the light hurt them. We stopped at the traffic lights and she looked at the side of the road where some men were working with shovels. 'I can't see what they're digging,' she said. 'That shows my eyes are bad.'

Suddenly my patience snapped and I shouted at her, 'I can't see what they're digging either. My eyes are not good, I need to have a corneal transplant soon, but I don't talk about it all the bloody time.'

She looked astonished that I should raise my voice at her and said huffily, 'I'd forgotten about your eyes.'

She was silent for a while, and I thought to myself, perhaps I should stand up to her more often. But when I dropped her off at her place, she clung to me with tears in her eyes and said, 'Don't stop loving me; you're all I've got.' I hugged her and when I felt her frail little body in my arms I felt sorry for her, and sorry for myself. Where had my lovely mother gone, the one who was always happy and smiling?

Later that week I had dinner with three women friends. We drank red wine and relaxed. The conversation turned to our elderly mothers. I told them about my mother's decline, and our visit to her retirement home to show off the baby.

'She wasn't like this when she was younger,' I said. 'I think it's a new stage. The onset of salinity, I mean senility.' We all burst out laughing.

Tamara, whose mother was blind and not easy, said, 'I'm taking my mother to Noosa on Sunday for a week in the sun.'

'A week,' I shrieked. 'You're a saint, how will you manage?'

She grinned, 'We'll take a bottle of gin.'

I admired Tamara's calm. She was single, and an only child. Tamara lived in Asia for years, running her own business in Bangkok. Now that her mother was old, she had come back to Melbourne to look after her. Her mother refused to move into a 'home' and relied on Tamara all the time, but Tamara did not complain. I felt guilty and disloyal whingeing about my mother, but it was a relief to share the problem with friends who were in a similar situation.

Leah said, 'I know all about senility, my mother has Alzheimer's. She's in Sydney, and when I visit her I have to sleep in the same room. When I can't bear it, I sleep on the couch in the living room.'

She smiled and said, 'After dinner my mother always says, "I think I'll have a little Scotch before I go to bed." I say "good idea," and she has the Scotch and washes the glass and puts it away. Then a few minutes later she sits up and says, "I think I'll have a little Scotch before I go to bed." I say "good idea," and she gets out the glass and has a Scotch, and washes the glass and puts it away. Then a few minutes later she says, "I think I'll have a little Scotch before I go to bed."'

We were all laughing now, imagining the scene. Leah said, 'After a while it's, 'I shink I'll haf a little shnifter before I go to bed.' She slurred and fell over the table, while we wiped tears of laughter from our eyes.

I looked at Angela and asked about her mother. Angela's mother was frail and lived in the country, two hour's drive away. Despite having a very demanding management job, Angela drove there every weekend to see her mother.

'She's in hospital, poor darling. She fell over and broke her pelvis.'

'What will you do when she gets out of hospital?' I

asked. Angela's mother had been living with her son and daughter-in-law on their farm.

'We don't know yet. She wants to go back there. She doesn't want to go into a home.'

It was a common story. Most of my friends' mothers did not want to go into a 'home' with other old people. They wanted to stay in their own place, or with their children. I thought how lucky I'd been, with my mother happy in her retirement home and in good spirits. Until now.

I looked at my watch. It was eleven p.m. 'I think I'll push off now,' I said. 'I've been with my mother all day and I'm tired.'

'All day,' said Tamara in surprise. 'What did you do all day?'

I hesitated. It felt very disloyal to be talking about my mother like this. They looked at me. 'You don't want to know, really, do you?' I say. 'It's so boring.'

'Yes, we do,' said Tamara. 'It's good to share it all, and your mother is the oldest, so it helps to know what's ahead.'

'Well, her glasses needed to be fixed, so I phoned her at breakfast and said I'd come over at ten a.m. I said I'd pick up the glasses, take them to the optician and then bring them back to her. I told her she could stay in bed and rest while I did that.'

I looked at them. 'Now, she normally doesn't get up and dressed until about eleven-thirty a.m. She has someone to help her shower and dress, and it takes a very long time. But when I got to her place at ten a.m. she was standing on the footpath waiting for me, fully dressed, with her make-up on, and a handbag on her arm like the Queen.' I mimed a shaking arm with a handbag on it.

'I said, "what are you doing here Mum, I told you to rest while I take the glasses". She said, "I know you don't want to see me, but I want to see you, I want to go out with you".'

Leah groaned and held her head. 'She's making you feel guilty.'

I grinned. 'You bet, and she must have got dressed like greased lightning. She said, "I didn't have a shower, I just dressed myself as quickly as I could." She got in the car and said, "It's so nice to get out of there, I'm so cooped up all the time. You're my rock; you're the only one I've got".'

Leah said, 'More guilt.' They all grinned.

I took a sip of wine and resumed my story. 'I got to the optician and gave him the glasses, and I bought her a coffee and that filled in half an hour, and then she said she wanted to buy a white blouse. I took her to about six different shops to look at blouses and she was rude to all the shop assistants. She said, "oh, I wouldn't wear that", or "what horrible little buttons, I couldn't do them up" or "that's cheapjack material".' I leaned over to Angela and fingered her blouse, rubbing the material between my fingers, imitating my mother.

'We went down the street and she leaned on me and we went into an exclusive shop which sold only blouses. She didn't like any of them, and then she said, "I feel dizzy without my glasses", and the shop assistant brought her a chair, and continued to bring her blouses, but she found fault with all of them. Finally Mum found a blouse which was okay and she asked how much it was, and when the woman told her, Mum said, "I don't feel like paying that much". I said, "why don't you try it on?" but she stood up and said to the shop assistant, "it's lunch time, we have to go now".'

'Of course it wasn't lunchtime, it was only eleven-thirty a.m. So we went back to the optician and the man said the glasses were not quite right. I asked him why not, and he said he gave the wrong order for the lens and could I bring them back on Tuesday and he'd do them again.' I looked at Tamara. 'That's how the morning disappeared.'

Leah looked sympathetic. 'Interesting how it's always the daughters who get sucked into all this, not the sons.'

I told her about my brother, on the other side of the world. 'He rang me a couple of nights ago and said "Mum sounds a lot better." She obviously puts on a brave face for him and saves up all the complaints for me.'

'Men are matter-of-fact,' said Angela. 'They don't put up with any nonsense. My sons would just say, "you'll be okay."'

'It's a feminist issue, isn't it?' I said. 'I keep thinking about third world countries where there are no nursing homes, and all those poor daughters and daughters-in-law have to look after elderly mothers day and night.'

'No,' said Leah. 'Our mothers would be dead in a third world country. It's only in western countries that we can keep them alive longer.'

She was right. I hadn't thought of it that way before. All those doctors and scientists were triumphant at finding new and expensive ways of keeping people alive, but they were not the ones who looked after them. My mother lived in a home full of elderly people, some with dementia, and she often said, 'They're keeping us alive too long.'

'How can we make sure we're not a burden to our children?' I wailed. Everyone smiled and nodded, but we didn't know the answer.

The next day a friend emailed to say that a man we all knew, a psychiatrist in his seventies, had committed suicide. He had motor neurone disease and faced a long, slow decline. It seemed brave, and yet, unthinkable. Then I thought about my baby grandson, whom I would see later in the day. He was my antidote to these gloomy thoughts; he was the new generation. When I held him and kissed his warm little head and saw him smile up at me, my irritation with my mother dissolved, and I was filled with peace again.

12

Mum's stroke

'My duty to her was conflicting with my duty to the rest of my family, and somewhere, fighting for space, was my duty to look after myself.'

When I told my sister Carina about my difficulties with Mum, Carina correctly diagnosed that Mum was afraid. She was afraid of losing my attention, afraid of losing her sight, afraid of being ninety-five and not knowing what horrors lay ahead. She was not afraid of death – she'd told us many times that she'd had a wonderful life and was 'ready to go,' but she was afraid of how it would come. She'd always thought she would go to sleep and not wake up, but now it seemed that it was going to be a long and gradual decline.

Carina rang her frequently with love and 'counselling' which seemed to help, and soon the antidepressants prescribed by the doctor took effect and Mum became more cheerful. She resumed her activities in the retirement home and I was able to cut back my visits to twice a week.

I was now able to get back to my writing, but at first it was very difficult. There had been a long gap while I was busy with Caleb and my mother. I sat at the computer and thought about a friend's joking phrase, 'It's easy to write, you just stare at the screen until your head bleeds.' At first I couldn't retrieve the memories of that long-ago love affair in Paris. I couldn't get the mood or the flow of words. I discovered there was only one solution and that was to just start writing.

At first I'd slouch along stumbling and tripping, but gradually it would improve and then miraculously I'd find myself jogging along, deep into it. I consulted old diaries and letters from my time in Paris and used them to recapture the mood. I found it therapeutic to re-examine this story I'd buried for so long. At fifty-nine, it was becoming clear to me that writing about the past was somehow a necessary spring cleaning before I could move into the next phase of life. I wrote every morning that I was free, and by the end of the winter I had completed over 30,000 words. The story had a clear shape in my head and I felt that if I could continue without interruptions I might finish it by the end of the year.

But then my mother became ill again. It started one morning early in September when I had a call from Eleanor, the manager of the retirement home. 'I'm afraid your mother's had another fall,' she said. 'It happened about three a.m. when she went to the toilet. She's got a large bruise on her behind and a deep cut on her arm. Her ribs are sore and the doctor's coming to see her later today.'

I left home immediately and found Mum in bed, pale and shaky, with a bandage on her arm. 'Oh thank goodness you're here,' she said. 'When I fell over, I cut

my arm somehow, and watched the blood pouring out.
I crawled across the floor to get to the bell.' She pointed
to a long streak of blood across the carpet. 'When I got to
the bed I couldn't reach the bell, so I crawled to the door
and grabbed the wooden door-stopper and banged on
the door until someone came. They told me to stay in bed
for a few days.'

She rolled over and lifted her nightdress to show me
a black bruise covering most of her buttocks. I kissed
her forehead and said carefully, 'Mum, there's a bell by
the toilet, you could have used that. And shouldn't you
be using your walking frame when you get up in the
middle of the night?' She didn't answer. She'd fallen
several times in the past two years. As soon as she
became more confident on her feet, she stopped using
the walking frame. I held her hands and thought, *it will
happen again.*

That evening, when I was about to cook dinner,
Eleanor phoned again. 'I'm afraid your mother's had a
small stroke,' she said. 'It has affected her right side. After
lunch her doctor came to check if she had any broken ribs
from the fall last night. While he was there, her speech
became incoherent and she lost the feeling in her right
arm. He called an ambulance immediately. She's in
casualty, you can go there straight away.' She named a
large hospital in the eastern suburbs, about forty minutes
from my home.

I stopped cooking and rushed to the hospital. Inside
casualty, it was the usual jumble of bright lights and loud
noises. Patients and relatives sat around worriedly, waiting
to see the doctors. The television blared away and small

children wailed. Doctors, nurses, ambulance drivers and cleaning staff bustled about.

I was used to these places now, so I went straight to the inquiry desk and helped fill out forms about my mother, then went through to the maze of small cubicles divided by curtains. I found Mum lying on a trolley, tucked in with a blanket, dozing peacefully. I kissed her and she opened her eyes and smiled. She tried to speak but only a jumble of sounds came out.

'I can't understand you,' I said, 'you've had a stroke and it's affected your speech.'

She tried again, then giggled and closed her eyes. 'Well, at least she's happy,' I thought, 'They must have given her a shot of something pretty good.' I found a young female doctor who told me they'd done a brain scan and found that it was not a major stroke. They'd also done x-rays on her ribs and there were no fractures.

'Her blood pressure is high, but we can't lower it because that might cause another stroke,' she said. 'What I have to do now is try to find her a bed in a private hospital. She does have private health insurance doesn't she?'

'Yes, full cover.'

'I'll let you know when we find a bed.'

I went back to Mum and held her hand while she dozed, then went out into the waiting room to see if I could find anything to eat. There was nothing except a vending machine. I extracted a paper cup of warm tea and a large, very hard biscuit. I took them back to the cubicle and pulled up a chair next to Mum's trolley. From time to time she opened her eyes and tried to talk, but it was incoherent.

I went for a walk and passed a glass-walled room where the doctors sat at desks, filling out forms, looking at computer screens and talking on the phone. Most of them were very young. I returned to my mother and sat with her again, holding her hand and smoothing her brow. By eleven p.m. I was weak with hunger and worry. Would Mum recover from this stroke or would she remain unintelligible? The young woman doctor appeared in the doorway. 'I'm sorry for the delay,' she said, 'but I haven't been able to find a bed for your mother so far. I'll keep trying.'

Just before midnight the doctor finally found a bed. 'It's in Riverview Private Hospital,' she said and gave me the address. 'Your mother will be in the care of Dr Stone, a consulting physician to the hospital. The ambulance will be here shortly.' I told Mum what was happening and that as it was late; I was going home and would see her in the hospital the next day. She seemed to understand.

First thing next morning, I phoned my brother in Spain and my sister in northern NSW. They were worried, and we agreed to talk again each day. Dr Stone, the physician at the private hospital, phoned me to say he'd examined Mum and was giving her pethidine because she had some pain from the fall. He said the stroke was small and might resolve itself with time.

It might, I thought, but how long can she go on having falls and strokes when she's ninety-five? I thought about my father, who at eighty-five had a small stroke and then a major one from which he never recovered. He had a horror of being hooked up to a life support system, with no quality of life. He and my mother were members of the

Voluntary Euthanasia Society and had given me and my brother and sister medical power of attorney, with instructions to refuse treatment if necessary. I explained this to Dr Stone and said that my mother did not want to become a 'vegetable' in a nursing home. He said he understood.

Riverview Private was half an hour away; a small hospital surrounded by trees and suburban houses. I found Mum in a ward with three other elderly women. Her speech was still incoherent and she was confused. The stroke had made it hard for her to swallow and at lunchtime she managed only a few mouthfuls. I fed her like a baby with a teaspoon and scooped up the food as it dribbled down her chin. When she was resting, I went to the reception desk and asked the nurses to note on my mother's forms that I had medical power of attorney and that she didn't want to be treated if it would mean ending up with no quality of life.

The next day her temperature went up. She tried to speak but only jumbled words came out. A nurse gave me a glass of water with a painkiller dissolved in it, and asked me to give it to my mother. She tried to swallow but it went the wrong way and she coughed and spluttered, trying to get her breath back, her eyes panicky. That afternoon, Dr Stone said she was dehydrated and ordered an intravenous drip.

I sat with her while she slept. In the bed opposite, there was a very old woman with white hair who slept all day with her mouth open and occasionally snored. The nurses said she was not expected to live long. In the bed next to Mum was another old woman who had had a stroke and did not speak. I felt surrounded by death and decay and wondered if Mum's life would end soon too. Watching these old women in their last stages made me think about my own mortality, and how much we take life for granted.

I wondered how long all this would last. The following week I was due to go on a holiday to Byron Bay in northern NSW. It was a beautiful part of Australia and Race and I had planned a special holiday to celebrate our thirtieth wedding anniversary. We were taking the entire family – our five children, those of their partners who could get away, and the seven grandchildren – fifteen of us in all. I wanted to go desperately, but what about Mum? I looked for a nurse and asked about the prognosis. 'It can take months to recover your speech after a stroke,' she said.

I drove home, pondering this. What if she did not recover though, and remained in this semi-vegetative state? So much for her wishes about not being kept alive. All we could do now was to take things day by day and see what happened.

The next afternoon I went straight to the ward and gasped with fright when I saw her. She was in a chair by the bed, slumped sideways with her mouth open. A small oxygen mask over her nose had slipped off and there was dried blood on her lip. 'Mum!' I cried, but she didn't recognise me and stared blankly ahead, her face pale. I ran back down the corridor to the nurses' desk.

'My mother,' I gasped, 'she's declined terribly – someone should have phoned me.'

The nurses glanced at each other and ran back to the ward. We found Mum having a seizure, her body jerking and thrashing around, her mouth open, gasping for air.

'Get her on the bed,' said one of the nurses, and they lifted her up and lay her down and put back the oxygen mask. Gradually the spasms weakened and she lay peacefully with her eyes closed. The nurse turned to me with a worried look. 'She wasn't like this before, I assure you.'

'It's okay. I just got a fright when I walked in.'

They tucked her in and left the ward. I sat down and spoke to her, but she didn't respond. From time to time she raised a shaky hand and tried to remove the oxygen mask which was bothering her. Each time I took her hand away and replaced the mask. I sat there listening to the gentle hiss of the oxygen. I wondered what was happening. Was she going to die?

An hour later she had another seizure. Her body started convulsing again, her mouth opened and her tongue poked out. This time the head nurse was in the ward and helped Mum until the fit passed and she was calm again. Afterwards, in the corridor, I asked her what was happening.

'She's having seizures because of the stroke,' she said gently. 'We've told Dr Stone and he'll be coming in soon. Have you told your family what's happening?'

'Yes. My brother's in Spain and my sister's in NSW. I'm keeping them up to date.'

'The best thing is just to hold her hand until it passes. You can talk to her if you like.'

Tears sprang to my eyes. 'But she doesn't seem to know I'm here.'

'Oh we don't know that. They can often hear you, even though they don't respond.' She put a hand on my arm. 'She's ninety-five, isn't she? The next fit could be her last.

On the other hand, she could be like this for days, or she could rally.'

'You mean she could recover from the stroke?'

'It's possible, although it seems less likely at present.'

Later that afternoon Dr Stone examined her and answered my questions. He was kind and patient. 'The fits are related to the stroke,' he said. 'In addition, her lungs are now infected and she has pneumonia. We're going to put some medication in the drip to help stop the fitting, and some antibiotics to ease the infection. The nurse will also give her Panadol suppositories to help lower her temperature. We're just trying to make her comfortable.'

I tried to absorb all this and said, 'Is she in pain?'

'No, she's not in discomfort, even when she's having a fit. Patients don't know about it when it's happening. It's more distressing for us than for them.'

At dinner time her chest was more infected and her breathing was very noisy. From time to time she stopped breathing altogether and I felt my own breath stop until she snuffled and rattled and started breathing again. A nurse put a long tube into her mouth and sucked out some phlegm which seemed to be trapped in her throat. By seven-thirty p.m. I felt exhausted and tearful and couldn't bear to listen to her laboured breathing any more. I'd been there all afternoon and had eaten nothing more than a biscuit and cup of tea. I told the head nurse I was going home and asked her to phone me if anything changed dramatically.

'There may not be time for you to get here,' she said. 'You've done all you could. It must be hard for your brother and sister, so far away and not able to say goodbye to her.'

'Yes,' I said and felt my eyes fill with tears.

'Have you got someone at home?'

'Yes, my husband.'

I got in the car and started crying. Mum's going to die, I thought. Her time has come. When I got home, Race had the dinner ready and we discussed what had happened and I cried again. After dinner I telephoned my brother and sister. They felt helpless at being so far away and wanted every detail. 'This is what she wanted,' they said, 'to go quickly and not become a vegetable.' I asked Race to phone the rest of our family.

As soon as I woke the next morning I phoned the hospital. They said Mum had had another seizure during the night, but was unchanged. I felt shaky again. On the way to the hospital my stomach clenched and I wished I did not have to go there. Mum was asleep on her back, snoring gently. The nurse told me to wake her up by speaking to her loudly.

I put my lips close to her ear and said, 'Mum, it's me.' To my surprise she opened her eyes a little and tried to smile. I kissed her and said I'd stay and she went straight back to sleep. I went to the visitors' lounge and made tea and stared out the window. Beyond the car park there were trees and houses and a blue sky. It was a beautiful September day, bright and colourful, while inside the hospital everything was white and pastel.

It looked like things might go on longer than expected, so later in the morning I went to her retirement home to collect some clean nighties. As I entered the building, I saw one of her friends walking heavily towards me, with a stick. 'How is your mother, dear?' she said. 'We've all been so worried. We miss her terribly. The life and soul has gone out of the place.'

It was true. She was always so full of life, the one who was into everything. When she was well she had loved the retirement home, just as she had loved boarding school. In both places she'd been the most popular girl. I explained my mother's condition and went to her room. Once inside, I was hit by sadness. It had been her happy little home for six years and it was full of her personality and the love that surrounded her. She'd chosen this room when my father died and it was filled with sunlight, looking out on the garden.

I walked closer to the desk and examined the objects on top. A vase of flowers, a small sculpture of 'Diana the Huntress,' photos of all of us, including the photo of her and Caleb, and a row of pretty cards from my sister who sent one every week with a message of love. On the small table between the chairs was a fax from my brother in Spain. The long stain of blood from the bathroom had gone miraculously and the bed had been stripped.

The room was silent and empty, waiting for her return, waiting for her to sit in her little armchair and watch television or invite a friend in for a drink or a cup of tea. I couldn't see her coming back to this lovely room or her happy life there. I fought back tears as I gathered up her nighties and put some things in a toilet bag and locked the door behind me. On the way out, I was stopped by Eleanor, the manager. 'Is there anything we can do for you?' she said, and her kindness made me cry. I drove away, wiping my eyes.

Back at the hospital, Mum was sleeping calmly and we

couldn't wake her. A nurse had cleaned her eyes, put Vaseline on her dry lips and swabbed her mouth with a lemony mixture. I opened the drawer by the bed and took out her wet nighties which smelled of urine and replaced them with clean ones.

Just before lunch Talya arrived, carrying Caleb. He was dressed in a little navy and white sunsuit and gurgled happily. Mum seemed to be almost unconscious, so we went to a nearby park. We had a picnic lunch and I cuddled Caleb and watched him feed at Talya's breast, his little hand spread out on her soft, creamy skin, and I felt my sadness easing away.

Later in the day we were joined by my stepson Sean, who was an intensive-care nurse. He tried to talk to Mum but she didn't respond, so we went into the sitting room and discussed the situation. It seemed to us that she could die from the pneumonia or another stroke or even starvation since she was unable to eat. On the other hand she might rally, but we were concerned that she might then be semi-paralysed and unable to speak properly.

The head nurse looked in and we voiced our concerns – that Mum didn't want to be kept alive in a paralysed state. Should we refuse further treatment? The head nurse was kind and reassuring. 'Dr Stone doesn't believe in prolonging life at any cost,' she said. 'He's a wonderful doctor. He's not giving her antibiotics indefinitely, just for a couple of days, to see if she picks up.'

After Sean and Talya left, Dr Stone visited Mum and she opened her eyes. He examined her and then joined me outside the room. 'Her chest is clearer and she's more peaceful,' he said, 'but her arm is still paralysed.' I asked if the treatment could restore her but leave her in a half paralysed state.

He said gently, 'We're not doing anything heroic here; we're just trying to keep her comfortable. We had to give her antibiotics, because she's conscious and it's not a nice feeling to have your lungs full of stuff, it's like drowning. We've also given her medication to reduce the swelling on the brain which was causing the fits. The swelling has subsided but she could still have another stroke. A lot of things could happen in the next few days. We just have to keep her comfortable and see what happens.'

I was grateful for his kindness, but confused and tired. Was she going to die or recover or remain somewhere in between? I went back into the ward to say goodnight. To my surprise, she opened her eyes and raised a shaky hand to her lips and blew me a kiss. When I got home, I phoned my brother in Spain. He was due to go to France for a week, and was wondering whether to go ahead or to fly to Melbourne. He said he couldn't sleep for worrying about Mum. We discussed the pros and cons and I said, 'She's not all that conscious and she can't talk. We don't know what's happening from day to day. Go to France and I'll call you on your mobile if anything changes.'

I slept badly, worrying about Mum, but the next morning when I phoned the hospital they said she was much better and was sitting up in bed having a wash. 'She's quite conscious now, but still can't swallow,' the nurse said.

I sat in bed thinking. I was exhausted by the emotional roller coaster of the past week and desperate to go on my holiday, which had been planned and paid for well in advance. My sister Carina was often unwell, but after six years of being the dutiful daughter looking after Mum I had had enough. Bugger it, I thought, it's her turn. I picked up the phone and told my sister I needed her to come to Melbourne and stay in our house and take over with Mum.

To my relief she agreed, and we discussed all the possibilities, including what sort of funeral arrangements to make if Mum went downhill again while I was away. I then phoned my aunt Dorothy, my mother's younger sister, who was ninety-four. 'I think your mother's time has come,' she said. 'We've all lived too long.'

In the afternoon I visited Mum and found her propped up on the pillows with the drip still attached. Her eyes were open but she did not recognise me. Her face was pale but more alive, and she had regained some movement in her right arm. Her speech was clearer, but she was talking to imaginary people in a confused way. I caught some odd words – '*old-fashioned bedspreads,*' and '*the green door*'. At one point she seemed to be talking to a man and said coquettishly, '*I'm only hinting,*' and laughed.

I leaned back in the chair watching her. Inside the room it was quiet, the other patients were asleep and the lights were dimmed. Outside it was warm. Sunlight filtered through shiny green leaves and bounced off hard surfaces. Canvas blinds had been lowered and a cool breeze came through the windows. It was a beautiful day. I heard Mum sigh and mumble to someone, '*I've slowed down, I'm just shuffling along.*' Then her speech became incoherent again.

That night Race took me out to a Vietnamese restaurant. He was loving and kind and supportive. I drank wine and started to feel human again and we discussed the approaching holiday. I told myself I must go, no matter what was happening to Mum, but I felt uncertain. What if she was dying and I was not there? My duty to her was conflicting with my duty to the rest of my family, and somewhere, fighting for space, was my duty to look after myself.

The next day I stopped for petrol on the way to the hospital. I was so distracted that I parked in front of another car, blocking its way. When I returned to my car the driver abused me loudly. I drove off, trying to concentrate, but my mind was distracted with Mum and getting everything ready for the holiday and my sister's arrival.

When I got to the hospital, I sneaked a look at the chart on the end of the bed and saw that the doctor had written, *'much improved'* and had reduced the anti-fitting dosage. I went to the nurses' station and they told me that Mum could swallow now and had sat up at lunchtime and eaten some soup and ice-cream. I went back to the ward and she was awake. I gave her some flowers and said, 'Do you know my name?'

She looked at me crossly and said, 'Of course I do, you think I'm mad don't you.'

I smiled and said, 'I hear you had some soup for lunch.'

'No, I had beautiful roast pork and some grapes.' She then went back to sleep, snoring quietly with her mouth open. A bit later she woke up and had an imaginary conversation in which she took a friend to a café and said, 'They make beautiful sandwiches here, what are you going to have?' Later on she started clapping, as though at a play, and burst out laughing. I heard her mention her sister's name and ask for her mother. A nurse came to change the drip and told me the hallucinations were probably caused by the chest infection.

The next day my sister arrived and I felt deeply relieved. We hugged each other and talked quickly. Mum had only been in hospital a week, but it felt much, much longer. I phoned Dr Stone and he said Mum's right arm and leg now had movement and her speech was improving. He said that when she could eat thick soup, they would take her off the drip.

In the afternoon, Carina and I went to the hospital and found that Mum was less confused. Carina had a long conversation with her and then fed her a bowl of soup, some ice-cream, apple juice and half a cup of tea. My sister was on a mission to get Mum well. I sat back and watched her putting a music player by the bed and making friends with the other old ladies in the ward. She'd worked with elderly people in the past and quickly found out about their ailments and their fears. She talked to the nurses and gave Mum a mouth swab. Soon Mum was smiling and to my amazement, I heard her ask Carina for another bedjacket and some nail-polish. I felt confused, but glad that everything was going well and I could have my holiday.

The next morning Carina went to the hospital alone and reported back excitedly that Mum ate her soup by herself and asked if she could have muesli for breakfast and braised beef for lunch, not realising that she could still barely swallow. After lunch the nurses got her out of bed and she walked to the toilet with their help. 'It took ages,' Carina said, 'but she did it, and we all clapped!'

I went to the retirement home and collected her bedjacket, nail-polish and walking frame. I took these to the hospital and said goodbye to Mum and in her croaky voice, she wished me a happy holiday. Carina said the nurses were calling Mum the miracle woman. 'Mum's so different to the other old people,' she said, 'she's asking the nurses their names and smiling at them – her old personality is emerging.'

I went home to pack my suitcase for Byron Bay. After dinner Race and I stayed up until midnight showing Carina how to work all our electrical appliances – the burglar alarm, dishwasher, oven, washing machine, dryer, television, DVD and video players and the telephone answering machine. I went to sleep exhausted, but woke at three a.m. as I had every night for the past week and lay there with my mind racing. It looked as though Mum was getting better, but was she? At ninety-five, nothing was certain.

13

Byron Bay

'I wanted to grieve fully and to have this period over and resume my normal life and my writing, but I couldn't.'

Byron Bay was a very special holiday, a way of bringing together our large family to celebrate three decades of a marriage that had been through many ups and downs. We gathered at the airport in Melbourne – our children, partners and seven grandchildren, ranging from sixteen-year-old Cosima down to baby Caleb. We then flew to Coolangatta airport south of Brisbane, picked up rental cars and drove to a small hamlet inland from Byron Bay.

There, among rolling hills, dairy farms and macadamia plantations, we had rented a church which had been converted into a brightly coloured house large enough for our group of fifteen. The main body of the church was the living room with a long refectory table. Upstairs, the choir stalls had been turned into a mezzanine area where the older children slept.

At the back of the church was a large kitchen and above it were bedrooms, bathrooms and a separate studio apartment. The church was surrounded by a tropical garden and there was an outdoor eating area. A small room which had once been the vestry had been turned into a dress-up room packed with clothes, shoes and hats of every size, from small children to adults. We immediately decided to have a dress-up party on the Saturday night.

It was the first time we'd all been together on a holiday, and I soon realised to my delight that I no longer needed to organise anything. I was surrounded by competent adults who quickly arranged the shopping, cooking, outings and entertainment. They knew how worried I was about my mother and urged me to rest. Slowly I started to unwind and kept reminding myself to 'butt out' and enjoy being looked after. Race and I were given the best room upstairs with a balcony and a view of the hills beyond. We spent much of our time resting or reading until a grand-child came to tell us it was time for dinner, or to invite us for a trip to the beach or a walk in the bush.

Like all families, there was some sniping between some of the siblings. From time to time I'd come across one of the adults complaining about someone else's children, or that somebody was not pulling their weight with the dishes or cooking. But to my delight the mutterings never erupted into a row. It was the big blended family I'd always wanted – lumpy in parts, but still together and doing their best to make the holiday a success.

Caleb at four months was the centre of attention. When he woke at 6.30 each morning, Talya brought him into the living room and handed him to whoever was awake. The older children played with him, and I heard his delighted gurgles downstairs as I lay in bed. Even at that early hour, the sun was already hot outside our window. Race and I discussed what we would do for the day and then Caleb was brought to us for a cuddle. He lay on our bed and laughed and kicked his legs in the air as we played with him.

There was no phone in the church, so I spoke to my sister on my mobile phone or walked up to the public phone box nearby, outside the volunteer fire station. On the second night away, when I phoned the hospital after dinner, Carina told me she had been there for eight hours without a break.

'I'm really worried about Mum,' she said. 'She's unhappy about everything and says she hasn't slept. She won't eat her meals and she's restless all the time. I've been waiting all day to see the doctor, but nobody seems to know when he's coming.'

'You can't do such long shifts at the hospital,' I said, 'you'll exhaust yourself. You're a terrible worrier, like Dad was.'

'I know, but I have to feed her at mealtimes because the nurses are too busy. They have so many old people to look after and if I don't stay, Mum won't eat anything.'

'Try not to be a perfectionist. She'll go up and down. You can't make all her problems go away.' We spoke at length, and when I got back to the house I had insomnia again.

The next day Mum was very tired and confused and sometimes hallucinating. She was eating very little and Carina said, 'I have to build her strength up.'

'For what? What sort of life is she going to have?'

'Well, she's not going to die, so we have to get her better.'

On the day of our dress-up party, Mum got worse. Carina phoned me late in the afternoon and said, 'When I got to the hospital she was slumped in her bed. I had taken a balloon and a lei and some barley sugar to cheer her up. I sang her theme song, "*Five foot two, eyes of blue,*" and said, "It's party time!" But she was too confused to respond. She couldn't walk to the bathroom today or sit up in a chair. She's like a zombie, it's almost like another little stroke. She talks, but it doesn't make much sense.'

Carina sounded stressed and emotional. I tried to console her but I was worried too. I hung up as seven-year old Felix came into the bedroom, wearing a pirate costume. 'Have you got your dress-ups?' he said excitedly. 'The party's going to start soon.'

When we came down the stairs, there was much laughter and clapping. Race wore a psychedelic 'rave' top and I had found some blue lurex trousers and a matching feather boa. We looked at the others. My stepdaughter Jane and her daughter Cosima wore long evening dresses. Fifteen year old Hagan wore a brown velvet cap and jacket while his eleven year old sister Georgia wore a silk dress and a tiara. Our tall son Keir entertained the children in red and black trousers and a cowboy hat. Caleb wore a tiny black devil suit with little horns and a tail.

For our special party we started with champagne. Then our son-in-law Martin brought in a platter of fish cooked with herbs on the barbeque and his son Sebastian followed with roasted vegetables. My stepdaughter Vanessa and her daughter Rebecca followed with wine and salads. Later on, the children carried in a large cake with thirty candles. Race and I blew out the candles and made some brief speeches. I told my three stepchildren that if it were not for my first meeting with them thirty years earlier, I might not have married their father. 'He was so formal and so involved with his work, that I was not sure what he was really like,' I said. 'But when I went to your house and saw what normal and friendly kids you were, I felt at home.'

Race smiled and thanked me for taking on his three children after their mother died, and said how lucky we were to be married all these years. We toasted each other and kissed, and the audience cheered. Jane, my older step-daughter, whispered to me: 'I'll bet you're surprised you made it this long,' and I said, 'you bet,' and we smiled at each other. Then we drank more toasts and the laughter and talk got louder. After dinner the children played their favourite CDs and we danced until late in the evening. Then, when the younger ones were sleepy, Race and I took them upstairs to their rooms while the others continued to talk quietly round the dinner table. Race and I then curled up in bed looking at the stars through the window and felt ourselves blessed.

The next day I got regular phone calls from my sister. Mum slipped in and out of consciousness and found it hard to drink anything. She stopped eating and slept a lot. I thought about her constantly as we drove to Byron Bay and climbed up the path to the lighthouse and saw dolphins swimming below. We went swimming and had a picnic on the beach, but I was only half present.

Carina phoned in the afternoon and said, 'I think Mum wants to end it all, because she doesn't want to stick around without a good quality of life. The nurses say it's unlikely she'll make a big recovery now at her age. The doctor says if she won't eat or drink, he'll have to consider putting the drip back in.'

This was a crucial issue for us. Mum had given us the power to refuse medical treatment. What if we agreed to put the drip back in and she remained in a zombie-like state, which she always said she didn't want? What would she want us to do? Carina and I discussed this at length. Carina then phoned my brother in Spain and talked with him and phoned me back. After dinner I stood in the public phone box in the warm night air and she told me that she and my brother thought we should not have the drip re-inserted.

I knew what this meant. If Mum could not swallow liquids she would slowly die, but we would ensure that she had enough morphine and sedatives to ease any pain or discomfort. Carina said she had spoken with the head nurse and the doctor and they would act on our wishes. 'Kelvin and I think we should let nature take its course,' she said. 'We should no longer intervene in any way, even with a drip. What do you think?'

Now that I was asked my opinion, I was suddenly confused. There were so many things we did not know about Mum's situation and we were all tired and stressed and it was hard to think clearly. I spoke at length with Carina and the head nurse, who was immensely kind. I found myself crying and I said to the nurse, 'I'm leaving it all up to you and Carina, you know what Mum wants and I trust you both.'

The next day, Carina phoned every few hours. We expected the end to be a few days away, given Mum's weak state and the fact that she would not eat or drink, except for the odd sip of water. They had not re-inserted the drip. I woke every night at two a.m. and lay there until five a.m. feeling stunned. My mind teemed with all the things that needed to be done when she died, such as organising her funeral, cleaning out her room and arranging her finances.

Carina was not sleeping either and was becoming very stressed. She phoned some of our close friends and relatives and organised a roster of people to sit with Mum throughout the day and evening. On the last night of the holiday, I walked up to the phone box and called Carina at the hospital and asked her to pass the phone over to Mum. If Mum was going to die soon, I wanted to talk to her before she went.

'Hello,' I said and imagined her curled up in the hospital bed, tiny and shrunken. There was silence at the other end. 'I love you very, very much,' I said into the void. 'You've been the best Mum ever.' There was a garbled noise at the other end. 'I can't understand what you're saying,' I pleaded. There was another incoherent noise. Carina took the phone and said she thought Mum was saying, 'God bless you.' I told Mum about our holiday and that we were leaving the next day. Then I hung up and cried as I walked back to the house. I felt sure she was going to die soon and I was glad I would be home to see her before it happened. It seemed right that she should go now, at the age of ninety-five and after a major stroke, and I felt a sense of relief mixed with sadness.

The next morning when I was packing up to leave, Carina phoned. 'You won't believe this,' she said, 'but I've just come into the hospital and Mum's sitting up in bed, smiling. She's eaten a bit of chocolate cake and she's drinking apple juice.'

'What?' I couldn't believe it. 'You mean we went through all that agony about not putting the drip back in, and she's turned around?'

'Yes. The doctor came in this morning and he was amazed too. He spoke to her and was able to get her to swallow her anti-stroke pills.' Carina started laughing hysterically and after a moment I joined in. Mum had surprised us again. Carina said, 'Yesterday, I was sure she was going to die and I just cried and cried. Isn't she incredible?'

I asked for news of Kelvin, our brother. 'He's catching a plane to Melbourne tomorrow,' she said. 'He's very worried and not sleeping, like us. He decided to come, no matter what.' We decided that it was useless trying to predict anything with our mother's health.

When we returned to Melbourne, I went straight to the hospital. Mum was sitting up and smiled at me. I held her hand and she launched into an imaginary conversation with people from her past. She could speak more clearly now, but none of it made sense. I heard her mention her sister's name, and my father's name, and 'the war'. I was not sure which war she meant – she had lived through both the first and the second world wars.

I could see a marked change in the week I'd been away. She looked very old and frail, but her blue eyes were bright in her shrunken face, and they darted around as she talked to her imaginary friends. At lunchtime I fed her, one spoonful at a time, and she ate a bowl of soup and half a bowl of custard. After lunch, she walked with a nurse to the toilet and then got into bed and slept like a baby.

The next day, the nurses sat her up in a chair. She was so small that she slipped sideways until we propped her up with cushions. They had brushed her hair and put on some powder and lipstick and she looked a little better. She wore a nightdress with a long sleeved singlet underneath and a warm bedjacket. 'She feels the cold,' the nurse said, 'after all, there's nothing of her, really.'

I kissed my mother on the forehead and sat beside her. To test her lucidity, I asked how old she was. She whispered, 'a hundred and five.' I didn't correct her. I asked if she'd like to get back into bed and sleep, but she looked towards the next bed, where the old lady had visitors, and whispered, 'No, I don't want to miss anything.' She then fell asleep in the chair.

On the weekend, Kelvin arrived from Spain. Carina picked him up and he went straight to the hospital. He cuddled Mum and she gave him a big smile, but was confused about where he'd been. Carina showed him all the little jobs we were doing for Mum when the nurses were busy – cleaning her eyes which had become sticky, brushing her teeth, putting Vaseline on her lips, helping her to the toilet and back into bed. He was eager to learn, and handled Mum gently.

I looked at my brother and sister and felt a huge relief that they were there. We had hardly seen each other in recent years, but at this moment we were close.

The next day, Kelvin, Carina and I met in the hospital lounge for a long talk. We agreed that if Mum continued to improve, she would have to go into a nursing home. We decided to visit her in shifts and to have a 'war council' every afternoon to compare notes. It was great to have my brother with us. He was tall, fit and suntanned, full of energy and practical suggestions, while Carina and I were tired and Carina's health was suffering. We decided that when things settled down a bit, Carina would return to her home in NSW.

That night, Kelvin stayed at the hospital for nearly three hours and phoned to tell me how he got on. 'She ate a *huge* meal,' he said, 'but it took forever, she chews each mouthful about fifty times.' I laughed, picturing him sitting beside her, feeding her with a spoon. He was used to doing things quickly and efficiently. Visiting Mum was going to test his patience.

'She's very confused,' he said. 'She thinks she's in a luxury hotel and it's absolutely beautiful. I don't know what chemicals she's on, but I want some!'

He told me how he did all the little jobs Carina had showed him, taking out Mum's plate and cleaning her teeth, even rubbing cream into her arms and legs. 'That's great,' I said, touched by this gentle side of my brother that had emerged.

'I'd rather be doing something than just sitting there,' he said. 'When the nurse came in, Mum didn't want to take her anti-stroke pill. I said, "Take your pill or I'll stick it up your botty!"' He chuckled. 'The nurse looked a bit surprised, but Mum took the pill. Then she wouldn't drink her water. I said "Drink it up or I'll smack you!" and the nurse said, "are you paying her back for what she did to you?"'

I laughed and said, 'She didn't smack us, though, did she? She just got us to do what she wanted by being bloody determined.'

'Sure. I was just joking. I got her to drink up, anyway.'

I hung up and thought how good it was for Mum to have three children who all related to her in different ways. My brother had always been the glamorous one, flying in from the far corners of the world. He'd been the one who'd taken her out to expensive restaurants, made her laugh and charmed her friends and the staff in the retirement home. My sister was musical and emotional, sending love every few days by letters, cards, phone calls and poems and composing songs for her. I was the dutiful one, the sensible one, looking after her in Melbourne. These were the roles we developed in childhood and had carried through life.

In the hospital, Mum improved. She was lucid at times, but confused at others. 'There's a bee on your shoulder,' she said, while I was sitting next to her. There was nothing there, but she plucked it off and asked me to get a suitcase from an imaginary cupboard because she thought she was coming to stay at my house. She slept a lot or sat in a chair by the bed, totally dependent on others.

That night I lay awake, reflecting that in her present state, she was like a slightly retarded child. The mother we knew – alert and full of life and laughter – was gone. My mother was not dead, but nor was she herself. I feared that the person we knew had gone forever and I found myself grieving for her. I wanted to grieve fully and to have this period over and resume my normal life and my writing, but I couldn't. I had been looking after her for six years and taking her in and out of hospitals for the past two and I was tired. I thought guiltily that things would be much easier if she had not recovered from the stroke.

The following week she was examined by a doctor from the Department of Health and Ageing to see if she was eligible for a nursing home. He stood by her bed and said that she was. 'Eileen, you won't be able to go back to the place where you were living,' he said kindly. 'You need more care now; you need help to eat and go to the toilet and to walk. Do you understand?'

She'd always looked up to doctors, especially male ones, and became more lucid in their presence. 'Well that's natural, as you get older,' she said calmly. I filled out lengthy forms, and he said she could be moved as soon as we could find a place for her. I walked out to the corridor with him and said, 'This isn't the way she wanted things to turn out. In her family they live for a long time, but mostly die quickly, in their sleep. That's what she always thought would happen to her, not this gradual decline.'

'It might be difficult for her,' he said, 'but at least you have assets with which to make her comfortable.' It was true and I suddenly felt ashamed, knowing how terrible some nursing homes were for people without money. I thought of a distant relative I used to visit in a nursing home for pensioners. She shared a small room with four others, and the smell of urine hit you as soon as you entered the front door. Her eyesight was too poor for reading and she sat all day in her room, or in a small lounge room, with no entertainment except the television. But that old woman never complained and was touchingly grateful for any kindness shown to her.

I left the hospital and met my brother and sister in a café. It was now early October and we sat under bright umbrellas in the sunshine. I told them about the nursing home approval and the doctor's estimate of her medical condition. 'He said she has a faulty heart valve,' I said. 'It could be a problem if she exerts herself too much.'

'Perhaps we should get her to run around the block then,' said my sister. My brother and I looked at her in astonishment and then shouted with laughter.

'I thought it but didn't want to say it,' Kelvin said, and we laughed again. I felt relieved that we all felt the same way. We were all under strain, not knowing what lay ahead. Our emotions were raw and humour helped. We were not used to working together or even being in the same city. There had been some flare-ups already when we disagreed on the best way to care for our mother. But mostly we were collaborating well and felt unexpectedly close.

In the next few days, we met with a financial adviser to work out how to pay for the nursing home. We started visiting those within a reasonable distance from where I lived. We quickly discovered that the best ones were full up and had long waiting lists. In the hospital, Mum made some more progress and became less confused. But a few days later, when Kel and I were visiting a nursing home, Carina phoned me on my mobile to say Mum had had another 'turn.'

'She was bored today, so I got a wheelchair and took her around the hospital,' she said. 'We talked about the nursing homes and I told her she couldn't go back to her place. She seemed to accept that, but when she was back in bed, she had chest pains and became really distressed. The nurse had to give her oxygen.'

We went straight to the hospital. Mum was calmer

now, but very restless. The nurse said it was not a heart attack but the result of anxiety, probably because Mum realised she could no longer go back to her old life.

Kelvin, Carina and I went into the tea-room and Kelvin exploded at Carina. 'Why did you tell Mum she couldn't go back to her old place?' he said. 'I thought we weren't going to tell her yet. Aren't we meant to be working as a team?' My sister burst into tears and said, 'Mum had to know sometime, I'm doing my best you know.' They argued for a while and then calmed down. 'It's okay kiddo,' my brother said, 'we're all under stress.'

Later that night, when Mum was in the bathroom and the nurses lifted her nightdress, I saw that her legs were just like sticks, her buttocks sagged and her flesh was wrinkled. She held onto the nurses while they put on a large incontinence pad. She tried to make a joke about it, but the words got muddled. My eyes filled with tears at her indomitable spirit, and I went into the sitting room so she wouldn't see me cry. When I returned, she was swaddled tightly in the blankets like a baby, fast asleep.

When I got home, exhausted, Carina was waiting up for me. She was due to return to her home soon and was anxious about Mum. She said Kelvin and I needed to stay with Mum all day or she would sink into dementia, and that we should feed her every meal or she wouldn't eat. 'That's ridiculous,' I snapped, 'we can't be with her all the time.' We started arguing heatedly. Finally Carina burst into tears and said that Kelvin and I were ganging up on her and didn't love her.

I lay awake for hours that night worrying, and at three a.m. put a note under her door saying that of course we loved her. The next morning she emerged for breakfast bright and cheerful, ready to visit Mum. She thanked me for the letter and said, 'I think it's very healthy to have these outbursts from time to time, don't you? I forget them as soon as they're over.' I looked at her in amazement through my sleep-deprived haze.

Two days later, when I arrived at the hospital the nurses said that shortly after breakfast, Mum had fallen out of bed. 'We had the rails up on the side of the bed,' they said, 'but she climbed over them and fell onto the floor. The cleaner was going past and found her. Fortunately she didn't break any bones or have any bruises. We're checking on her every five to ten minutes, but we can't watch her all the time.'

I asked Mum why she climbed out of bed. 'I felt trapped,' she said. 'I can't get comfortable.' She moved constantly from side to side, threw the sheets off and put her bare legs up on the rails. I tried to calm her and played some of her favourite music, but she told me to turn it off. I got a wheelchair and took her to the sitting room, where she looked out the window and had a cup of tea. Gradually she calmed down and her head sank lower until she was asleep in the wheelchair. I took her back to the ward and the nurses put her into bed.

I spoke to Dr Stone, who said she was restless because she was becoming more alert and wanted to be doing more. He said she'd be better in the nursing home because they'd have activities during the day. I spoke to Kelvin and Carina and we decided to move her straight away to the only nursing home with a vacancy, Melbourne Lodge. It was a large nursing home like a luxury hotel. We preferred a smaller one called Yarra House, but it was full. We left her on the waiting list at Yarra House, and told Mum what we were doing and she seemed to understand.

That night, Race and I had friends to dinner. It was my first social event in a month. I felt exhausted, but it was good to talk and laugh with friends, and it turned out that they too had problems with elderly parents. One friend was looking for a nursing home for his mother and we compared notes. Another friend said her mother needed to be in a retirement home but refused to go because of her small dog.

The next day this friend phoned me to ask about funeral parlours. 'My mother wants to pre-pay her funeral,' she said. 'She's decided that when she dies she wants her dog put to sleep and cremated with her. She wants them both to be in a cardboard box, so as to save chopping down trees for a coffin.'

I laughed. 'I don't think they do cardboard boxes,' I said. 'But you might be able to get chipboard.'

My brother's partner, Lorraine, arrived from Spain after tidying up their affairs there. She was young and fit and full of kindness to us all. Mum was excited to see her, and happy about going to Melbourne Lodge because she was tired of the hospital.

Carina and I went to Mum's retirement home to sort through her belongings. We were in her room for hours, cleaning out her desk and discussing what to keep, what to give away and what to store at my place. We packed some clothes for Mum and chose some small items of furniture and ornaments to take to her new room in Melbourne Lodge. Our work was interrupted every few minutes by one of the staff or the residents coming into the room to ask how Mum was and to tell us how much they missed her. When we got home it was nearly midnight and I was so tired that I wished I could drop off the edge of the world for a couple of weeks.

14

Melbourne Lodge

'Each day I felt tired with all the anger I was bottling up.'

'A friend of mine says it's worse when your parents go into a nursing home,' my brother said. 'They become much more demanding and you just have to get used to it.' He was right. Mum had now moved into Melbourne Lodge, but she complained constantly. She'd made some recovery from the stroke and could walk slowly with her walking frame, but she hated being dependent. She missed the retirement home and her friends there, and sat by the window most of the day looking down on the car-park, waiting for one of us to arrive.

Most of the other residents were bed-ridden or had various stages of dementia. In the dining room everyone ate in silence. Mum tried to talk to them, but it was impossible. I sat beside her and cut her food into small pieces. She held her fork in her shaky right hand, but often the fork moved to her mouth with nothing on it or overbalanced and the food tumbled into her lap. She wore a large plastic bib and chewed each mouthful deliberately. I watched the other residents eating slowly and dropping their food, and listened to the background music which was always relentlessly cheerful. '*Chattanooga choo-choo, won't you choo-choo me home.*'

One afternoon there was a bus outing and I helped Mum get ready. A nurse took her to the toilet and then I brushed her hair, put on her lipstick, buttoned up her coat, put a clean hanky in her pocket and waved goodbye, just as I did to my children when they were small. When she returned from the bus trip, she said it was bumpy and she wanted to go to the toilet all the time and was definitely not going again.

Now that Mum was in the nursing home, my sister was able to return to her home in NSW. Our second bedroom was empty again and I set up my computer on the desk and wondered when I would ever get back to my writing. Looking after Mum was taking up most of my time. My brother Kelvin and his partner Lorraine were still in Melbourne helping and we took it in turns to visit Mum morning and afternoon, hoping she would adjust to her new situation. She blackmailed us emotionally and we found it hard to leave her when she was so unhappy and defenceless.

Mum complained of aches and pains which came and went mysteriously. The staff said it could take weeks to adjust to being in a nursing home and that imaginary ailments were common. One day Mum said sadly, 'I never wanted to end up like this you know, to be a worry to you all. I don't know what I'd do if you didn't visit each day.' She was coming to realise that her former life was over and she was trying to adjust, but she was always tired and nervy and anxious. She had always been fastidious about her appearance but now she dropped food and drink on her clothes all the time.

I went back to her room at the retirement home for a final clean-out. It was amazing how much had been packed into one small room. In the bathroom, I found jars of pills and medicines labelled by my father before he died six years earlier, and a hidden stash of sleeping pills because she was afraid of running out. In the chest of drawers, I found jewellery I hadn't seen since I was a child, a drawer of stockings and a drawer of belts and scarves of different colours, all chosen carefully to go with different outfits. There were hats, gloves and three umbrellas.

I climbed on a chair and looked in the top of the wardrobe. I took down four suitcases and in one I found bolts of silk materials waiting to be made into evening clothes. I ran my hand over these beautiful fabrics and wondered why she'd kept them. I remembered how she and I used to sew together when I was a teenager, and that when I left Australia in my twenties, she used to cry whenever she walked past the sewing machine. I remembered that when she was going to marry my father she made her own trousseau, with silk night-dresses and underclothes she embroidered by hand.

Inside the wardrobe there was a shelf of goodies for visitors – sweet biscuits, dry biscuits, chocolates, smoked oysters, coffee and tea, her hand-painted tea-set and some crystal glasses. She loved clothes and they hung neatly in categories – skirts, trousers, suits, blouses, dresses, all on individual hangers. I packed them all into cases and boxes to take away and then went through her desk – an archaeological dig of old photos, love letters from my father, bank statements from years back, a drawer full of bridge things and letters from friends and relatives.

As I worked into the night, the staff on duty dropped in to say hello. There was tiny dark Elena, who was Greek, and large, beaming Susan who was Fijian. 'Oh how we miss your mother,' they said, 'please give her our love.' Near midnight, on one of my many trips to the car with boxes, I found them having a cup of tea and I said, 'I'm still at it, Mum had so many clothes.'

Elena nodded and looked sad. 'I remember one day she had on white slacks and a pale pink silk shirt and a pink and white necklace. She came and asked me to do it up, and she looked so lovely.' I remembered my mother as she'd been then, beautiful and always smiling, and I could not speak.

When I made my last trip to the car, I thanked them for their kindness to my mother. Susan put her arm around me and told me to look after myself and to bring Mum back soon and they'd give her a special afternoon tea. I got in the car, tears in my eyes, full of admiration and gratitude for women like them. Night and day, they were giving love to old people, many of whom were very difficult. In exchange they got low pay and no status. How did they do it? I remembered one of them saying, 'It's like looking after little children. You have to be patient, and sometimes they give you love in return.'

In Melbourne Lodge, Mum continued to be depressed. She was bored, but she couldn't concentrate on anything but her own miseries. When it was my turn to visit, I found my stomach churning as I drove to the nursing home. The physical strain was nothing compared to the anxiety. I reflected that most of us are programmed to help our parents and do what they ask. If they're anxious, we're anxious. If they have a problem, we feel we should fix it.

'I hate being like this,' she said to me one day. 'I wish I'd just "gone" in the hospital when I had that stroke.'

'I know.' I felt that somehow we had failed her.

She mumbled something about death and said, 'If things get too bad, I can do something about it.'

'What do you mean?'

'You know – euthanasia.'

'Mum,' I said, 'it's actually very hard to implement. Unless you become very ill again, we can't refuse treatment.'

'What about a pill?'

I kissed her and said, 'No darling; that would be murder.' She became confused and said something I couldn't follow. It was difficult now to have a proper conversation with her about this or anything else.

My brother and I met with her local doctor to discuss the situation. He said her restlessness was caused by anxiety. We told him we were visiting her each day and he said we must cut down on our visits and look after ourselves. 'It's just like leaving a little child at kindergarten,' he said, 'It's hard, but you have to do it.'

We broached the difficult subject of our medical power of attorney, and her views on not prolonging her life. 'I understand that,' he said. 'She made her views very clear to me in the past.' I asked if he had any religious or personal views on withholding treatment. 'No, I don't have a problem with that,' he said, 'but you can't make rules about it, you have to look at it on a case by case basis.

If something happens to her again, I'll discuss it with you first before we decide what to do.'

We found this reassuring. Melbourne Lodge gave us a form to fill out called 'Final Life Decisions.' We said that if she had another medical emergency, we wanted her to be treated by her local doctor, who would consult with us as to whether or not hospitalisation was required.

My brother and I decided to stop feeding her at meal-times, even though she begged us to help her. The next day, Kelvin visited briefly and left when lunch arrived. When I came in the afternoon, Mum was in bed and said, 'Oh thank God you've come, I'm so unhappy. I didn't eat anything at lunchtime because Kelvin wouldn't stay, so I sulked. I loathe being in the dining room alone, no-one talks and it gives me the heebie-jeebies. When I ask the staff to feed me they say, "Oh Eileen you can do it".'

I arranged for her to have dinner in bed that night, and she ate a lot and mostly fed herself. I made myself a cup of tea and was just about to drink it when she wanted to go to the toilet. We pressed the buzzer, but no-one came. 'I have to go right now,' she said anxiously, 'you'll have to help me.'

I helped her walk to the toilet, took down her pants, and afterwards wiped her bottom. 'You're not bad for a beginner,' she said as I pulled her pants up again.

I laughed and said, 'I've wiped your bottom before,' and she flashed back, 'and I've wiped yours.'

When we got back to her room, she said, 'Oh, your tea has gone cold, you should have drunk it when it was hot.' I felt a flash of rage and thought; *you wouldn't have bloody waited, would you?*

205

Outside the door Rosie, one of the residents, stood in the hallway as she did every night, and called out, *'Yoo-hoo, yoo-hoo, is anyone there? Cuckoo, cuckoo, yoo-hoo.'* She was waiting for someone to put her to bed, but it was too early. She called out again, and knocked on her door loudly to summon the staff.

After ten minutes I couldn't stand it anymore and went outside. 'The nurses will be here soon, Rosie,' I said firmly, 'Go to your room and wait for them.' She turned her vacant, child-like face to me and said, 'Oh, do you think so?' and went in the direction of her room.

Five minutes later she was back in the corridor, yodelling. I spoke to her again. She looked at me and frowned. 'I never expected this you know,' she said. 'I'm not trying to be any trouble, why is this happening? What am I to do?' She walked into my mother's room and looked around vaguely. We invited her to sit down, which she did for a few minutes, then wandered into the hall to start yodelling again.

One morning I found Mum in the dining room with Margaret, the red-haired activities officer, and three other residents – Rosie who yodelled at night, Elaine and Maud. All three had some form of dementia. Margaret was an attractive woman in her forties who was full of fun and ideas, trying to bring life into the place. She laid out a card game based on Scrabble and tried to explain it. It was too complicated for them and I suggested she play it like 'Grab' or 'Snap' where they'd only have to find a pair.

She agreed and dealt out half a dozen cards to each person, and placed the rest of the cards on the table, face down. She turned up a card with the letter D on it, and said if they had a card with the same letter they should place it on top, and say Grab! Mum got the idea immediately, but the others were confused.

'What letter do you have in your hand?' Margaret said to them.

'I have a "D",' said Elaine.

'Wonderful,' said Margaret. 'There's a D on the table, put your card on top.'

Elaine giggled and did nothing. 'Put it on the table,' said Mum, but all Elaine could do was giggle. I thought it would be easier to teach a three year old. Margaret took the card gently from Elaine and put it on top of the other card.

Margaret turned up the next card on the table, a T. '*Tea for two, and two for tea*,' she sang, and Mum and I joined in: '*Me for you and you for me.*' Elaine and Rosie and Maud looked on in bewilderment.

'Has anyone got a T?' said Margaret. 'I have,' said Mum, and slammed it down with a 'Grab!' and we clapped her.

Margaret turned up a card with the letter U. '*If you were the only girl in the world*,' sang Mum, and to our amazement Rosie joined in slowly, '*and I were the only boy.*' Margaret and I clapped as Mum and Rosie finished the song. Rosie couldn't play the card game, but now for a moment, her long-term memory had come back.

'Where did you grow up?' I asked her, and she said, 'Johannesburg,' and spoke clearly about her childhood for a few minutes before becoming confused again.

We sang the song again, enjoying ourselves now. Maud had a card with U on it. We held her hand and placed her card on the table, and said 'Grab!' and clapped her, but she stared at us blankly. The next card was a J. '*Jack and Jill went up the hill,*' I sang and Mum and Margaret joined in. The next card was a Z and we couldn't think of a song, so Margaret launched into the kindergarten song, 'I'm a little teapot.' I sang it with her and we did the movements together, *I'm a little teapot, short and stout, here is my handle, here is my spout. When I get all steamed up, then I shout, just tip me over and pour me out.*'

'I'd like a penny for every time you and your sister sang that when you were little,' Mum said to me. Elaine giggled. Rosie smiled. Maud looked bewildered.

When the game was over, we packed up the cards and waited for lunch to arrive. Joanna, another resident, walked slowly towards the dining room with her walking frame. She stood in the doorway, dressed in black, and scowled at everyone. She had a form of dementia which made her pleasant one day and aggressive the next. 'Hello,' said my mother in a friendly way, but Joanna ignored her.

I said goodbye to Mum and got up to leave. A nurse took me aside and told me to walk quickly past Joanna. 'You're all right as long as she doesn't see your fear,' she said. It sounded like a mad dog. I slunk past, avoiding eye contact. Margaret followed me and said she was keeping an eye on Mum, because Joanna could be dangerous.

The next day, my brother found Mum very distressed. She said she was unable to get help to go to the toilet in the middle of the night and had lain in a wet bed. Kelvin spoke to the nurses and discovered that Joanna had gone berserk in the middle of the night, hitting out with a stick and trying to get into people's rooms. The two nurses on night duty had to guard her until she could be taken away and they could not attend to the other residents. They said Joanna would be sedated and would return in a week.

Mum complained every day now that she didn't like Melbourne Lodge and wanted to go to Yarra House, the smaller one. We explained that she was on the waiting list, but we couldn't speed up the process. She complained about the staff at Melbourne Lodge. Some were lovely, but some were not as good. One afternoon when I visited, she was very upset. 'I had a terrible day,' she said. 'I had a fight with a male nurse at breakfast, and I'm still shaking.'

'What happened?

'He was new and didn't know anything. He came in early and said loudly, "Wakey, Wakey," and was rough as bags when he was giving me a shower, and then he gave me cornflakes with steam coming off them. I said, "I have my cornflakes cold," and he said, "shall I put them in the fridge?" Can you imagine that?' she said crossly.

'I suppose he was trying to cool them down.'

'Don't be ridiculous, you can't cool down cornflakes once they're hot!'

I looked at her and thought he might have wanted to tip them down her neck. She was projecting her distress onto everyone else. I got out the photographs of my holiday in Byron Bay to show her, but she lost interest after one or two, and wanted to talk about her problems again.

'I loathe this place,' she said, 'I feel cooped up like a bird in a cage.' She said she dreaded filling in the time after lunch, and again after dinner.

'But you have lots of activities.'

'I don't like most of them, they're silly, and people tell me I'm the life and soul of things and I don't WANT to be the life and soul of things.' We sat there in silence for a moment and then she said, 'I'm sorry I'm like this, like a spoilt child.'

Yes you are, I thought, and went for a walk to get away from her. I ended up in an empty room further up the corridor and sat down, enjoying the silence. Suddenly she was at the door with her walking frame.

'What do you want?' I said crossly.

'Take me to the toilet.' I took her and when we were back in her room she wanted the TV on, but didn't watch it. She talked about her clothes, and said she was confused about what to wear each morning. I said she had too many clothes and I'd take some home. As I was sorting them out, she issued instructions over the noise of the TV about how to wash and dry-clean them.

'Are you watching TV or talking?' I said.

'Both,' she said crossly.

Each day I felt tired with all the anger I was bottling up. When the weekend came, Kelvin and Lorraine took over and Race and I escaped to the country for the day, to visit friends in Castlemaine. We had lunch outdoors and then visited a friend who was a keen gardener. We strolled around his garden in the sunshine and it was beautiful, full of Banksia roses, clematis as big as saucers, Californian poppies, pansies and petunias. I forgot about Mum and the nursing home and was happy.

The next day I walked on the beach with a friend and asked her advice about my mother. She was a widow who had visited her husband for years in a nursing home until he died. She said I should visit once a week and stay for an hour only. I knew that we should regain control of the situation. It would have been easier if Mum did not regard my brother and me as 'retired.' But we were not retired really, my brother had business interests and wanted to return to his life overseas, and I wanted to return to my writing. My friend said my mother was being manipulative, keeping us there. Yes she was, but I understood why. She was afraid and confused and no longer in control of her life.

A few days later I went to a function organised by the ACTU, my old workplace. It was good to see my former colleagues and to listen to rousing speeches about the problems of working people and the need for social change. I reflected that my best working years were at the ACTU and started to feel nostalgic for my old life. I wondered guiltily whether I should to some work in the outer world when my mother was better. But I knew that I wouldn't. I no longer wanted to go to meetings or give speeches or write submissions or do any of the things I once did.

Kelvin, Lorraine and I reduced our visits to once a day and took turns, so that each of us had one day on and two days off. On my first day off I felt liberated. I took Caleb to the Botanical Gardens and in the afternoon went to a yoga class, but I kept looking at my watch all day, wondering if Mum was all right. Kelvin reported that she complained constantly and asked to be moved to the other nursing home.

The next day it was my turn. I went in the evening and

helped with her meal and preparation for bed. When she was tucked in I kissed her goodnight like a child and she whispered, 'Thank you so much, all of you, for looking after me. I'll write to you from heaven.' I tiptoed out, wishing she could go to sleep and not wake up, the way she wanted.

15

Yarra House

*'I desperately wanted some uninterrupted days, a length of
time, like a roll of fabric, not little scraps.'*

When Mum had been in Melbourne Lodge for a
month we were contacted by Yarra House to say
there was a vacancy. My brother was excited. 'It's great,'
he said. 'This is what she wants. Now, perhaps she'll be
happy.' I nodded, but wondered whether anything would
make her happy again.

Yarra House was smaller and more homely than
Melbourne Lodge. Most of the residents were perma-
nently bedridden or in a wheelchair, but there were fewer
dementia patients. The carers were mature women who
had been there for a long time and were kind and patient.
Mum immediately liked it. On her first day she was
wheeled into the sunny garden and sat under an umbrella
with some of the other residents. They were listening
to one of the carers reading a book about the Australian
painter Norman Lindsay. Some were dozing, but one or
two were listening and seemed to understand.

Within a few weeks, Mum could move slowly around

the nursing home with her walking frame and started going to the toilet alone. I wrote to friends and relatives telling them she was in good spirits. We changed our visits from daily to every second day, and as we were doing it in turns, life started to return to normal. I began to catch up with friends and tackle the jobs I'd neglected while Mum was ill. I spent hours doing paper work for her – paying bills, claiming hospital expenses, doing her taxation, changing her address and filling out forms for the electoral office. I had not done any writing for months, but hoped to resume as soon as my other jobs were out of the way.

Two weeks later Mum developed a bladder infection and felt dizzy when she got up or lay down. My brother lectured her about going to the toilet without someone to help her, but the very next night she went to the bathroom alone and fell. She was taken by ambulance to a big hospital in the city and when we got there, we found she had broken her left hip vertically and horizontally and would need an operation. She was in the care of an orthopaedic surgeon and a general physician. She lay on a trolley, grinning at us, doped up with morphine.

'Oh, I'm such a trouble to you all, I don't know why you love me,' she said, and giggled like a naughty child. Then she remembered that my father was in the same hospital when he died of a stroke and said, 'It would be better if I could just pop off too.' My brother spoke to the physician about Mum's views on 'dying with dignity' and said if anything dramatic occurred in the operation, it would be better to let her go. The physician was under-standing and said they would not put her on a life support system, and if she had a heart attack during the operation they would not revive her.

Next day she had the operation and the surgeon said it was a great success. My mother's ninety-five year old hip was now held together with screws, a plate and a bolt. We were back to visiting daily and when the morphine wore off she became confused and anxious and wanted us with her all the time. Whenever I said goodbye she said, 'Don't leave me alone, it's terrifying here.' Sometimes she was vulnerable and child-like and even called me 'Mummy,' but at other times she was very demanding. My life was on hold again and I felt resentful. My brother and I phoned each other and complained about how difficult she was. Only Lorraine, my brother's partner, remained endlessly patient and kind.

Every night now I woke with the same dilemma – another day had disappeared without any writing. Writing was now my 'work' and without it I felt guilty and deprived. I couldn't write in snatches here and there; it wouldn't turn on and off at will. I desperately wanted some uninterrupted days, a length of time, like a roll of fabric, not little scraps. I lay there from two a.m. until five a.m. tossing and turning, turning and tossing. I was too hot and threw off the eiderdown. A bit later, I was too cold and put it on again.

My restlessness woke Race and he went into the next room to read. I threw off the eiderdown and took the blanket from his side of the bed and doubled it over mine. I turned over the pillow, got some hot milk, read for a while, tried sleeping again, but my mind wouldn't be still.

The problem was the conflict between my mother and

my writing. Where did my duty lie? To her or to myself? How did I get trapped like this, and what was the lesson? Should I rebel against parental pressure and stop being so dutiful? Or was the lesson that caring for a family member was more important than my own spurious 'work,' which could wait, after all?

My gut feeling was that if I resented the fact that I was with Mum so much of the time, I should back off a bit. I thought about my friends who were still in busy full-time jobs. Visiting grandchildren and elderly parents was something they did on the weekends. Something they fitted in around the edges of their lives, instead of it taking over. But I no longer had a paid job as my excuse. Writing was not seen as a job, but a hobby which could be put aside at any time.

After ten days in hospital, Mum went back to Yarra House. She was now confined to a wheelchair and was completely dependent. She needed help to be washed and to go to the toilet and couldn't even reach into the drawer by her bed or go to the cupboard to get a cardigan if she was cold. She had to press the buzzer to get help for every-thing and the staff couldn't come straight away because they had other people to attend to, and the waiting drove her crazy.

She complained that she was bored, but she couldn't concentrate enough to read or watch television or listen to talking books. She sat in her wheelchair in the lounge-room every afternoon with the other old people or slept. She liked it when someone came to sing or play the piano, but she couldn't do the craft activities because she'd lost dexterity in her hands. She, who always laughed and talked non-stop, was now subdued and rarely smiled. She was on anti-depressants, but the doctor did not want to increase them for fear of making her more confused and falling again.

My sister asked her on the phone, 'On a scale of one to a hundred, where would you be in terms of happiness?' Mum said, 'Two out of a hundred.' My brother visited and found her in bed crying. She said she wished she'd gone quickly instead of lingering on like this. He told her she was going through another adjustment process and she calmed down.

My sister phoned and emailed every few days to give us support. She had experienced ill-health and depression herself in the past and said Mum's low spirits were related to fear. 'All her life she's been in control and a perfectionist about everything,' Carina said, 'but now she's struggling to have any control over her environment, which makes her more afraid. It might be hard for her, but it's very hard for you too. It's well known that people in her situation take it out on their carers and loved ones. You have to look after yourselves, as well as look after her.'

My brother and I wondered how long Mum would go on. Some of the old ladies in the nursing home were over a hundred years old. Could she possibly live that long, another five years? Her older brother had died just before his ninety-sixth birthday and her younger sister was ninety-four, still living independently. They had an aunt who lived to a hundred. It seemed that although her body was becoming frailer and her mind was sometimes confused, there was nothing to stop her going on for years.

If nature had been allowed to take its course she

probably would have gone by now, but nature was no longer allowed to take its course. She took pills to prevent her having a stroke, pills to keep her blood pressure down, pills to stop her blood clotting, pills to help her sleep, pills to stop constipation and pills for depression. Nor was she likely to fall again, now that she was confined to a wheel-chair or a day-bed.

I had started focussing on articles in the newspapers about ageing and death. A senior research scientist in Sydney, Professor Tony Broe, said that for people over eighty there was less risk of chronic disease, but an increased likelihood of diseases of the mind such as Alzheimer's, Parkinson's or dementia, as systems in the brain broke down. My mother was often confused now and I feared that her mild form of dementia would get worse.

Scientists said we were going to live longer and longer, and most of them seemed very excited about it. They said the average life expectancy for men had increased from fifty-five years of age in 1910 to seventy-eight now, and the average life expectancy for women had increased in the same time from fifty-nine to eighty-four. They said in a few decades, the average life expectancy could be over 100. Progress would be made with diseases associated with ageing such as arthritis, diabetes, cardiovascular problems, Alzheimer's and cancer. Parents-to-be would select embryos that bore longevity-promoting genes.

I wondered about all this. Younger people wanted life to go on forever, but older people like my mother, who'd faced up to their mortality, were not afraid to die. They were more afraid of *how* they would die, and of living too long without a proper quality of life. Medical science could prolong a person's life, but in some cases it was better not to.

Now that I was faced with my mother's mortality, I had to think about my own. One night I came home from the nursing home and said to Race, 'My mother doesn't want to be alive any more, but she could go on for years. How can you and I avoid this happening to us when we're old?'

'If I have a stroke, just make sure they don't revive me,' Race said.

'It's not that easy,' I said, 'look what happened to Mum. When she had the first big stroke, we explained her wishes to the doctor, but he gave her medication for the fits and the pneumonia and she recovered. Then we went to Byron Bay and she went downhill again. We asked him not to intervene any more and he agreed not to, but she recovered by herself. The same thing could happen to us. In the case of a stroke or Alzheimer's, we could linger on for years in a nursing home.'

Race and I did not want to be a burden to each other or to our children. Race's particular fear was of suffering 'locked in' syndrome like the French writer Jean-Dominique Bauby who became completely paralysed, but was still conscious and rational. He could only blink his left eyelid, and used this to communicate and dictate his book, *The Diving Bell and the Butterfly*.

We had given each other and our children the power of attorney to withhold medical treatment, if we could no longer make those decisions for ourselves. But after my mother's experience, we realised this was not enough. We also needed to make our wishes very clear through an 'advance directive' or 'living will.' We planned to give this to our children and to our G.P. and if we had a life-threatening illness, to every doctor who treated us. In the case of a stroke like my mother's, we would refuse all treatment except sedatives and painkillers.

Voluntary euthanasia was becoming one of the contentious issues of our generation. Race and I discussed it with friends and agreed that we wanted to work out a way to end our lives when our quality of life deteriorated too much, but apart from refusal of treatment, how would we do it? Race said, only half-jokingly, that we needed a prussic acid pill like the Nazis had in a pouch around the neck, which some of them used when the war ended.

In the newspapers, there were numerous articles about Philip Nitschke, an Australian doctor who advised people how to end their lives. Ending your own life was legal, but helping another person was a crime. There were a number of reports of people ending their lives when they were terminally ill, or choosing a time to go before their health deteriorated too badly. But not everyone could do it – a friend told me about an old woman in Melbourne who managed to get hold of a suicide pill and invited her friends to her house to say goodbye, put on her best night-dress and her favourite music, then could not go through with it.

When I thought about my mother's experience it seemed that none of this was clear cut. If she became very ill again, we would discuss the situation with her doctor and try to keep her out of hospitals. In the meantime, all we could do now was to give her love and support. Kelvin, Lorraine and I tried hard to cheer her up. We saw her every few days and some family friends, Des and Andrée, visited her on Sunday mornings. We took her for walks in her wheelchair and sometimes for a drive. Slowly she seemed to become calmer. One day after I had wheeled her back into the nursing home, I asked her to stand up and hold on to me while I took off her coat. She put her arms around me and I gave her a cuddle and said 'I love you.'

'I love you too,' she said, and got a bit teary.

'I feel so sad for you in this situation,' I said, 'you never wanted to be like this, did you?'

'No never. I don't like it, but I don't know how to end it, short of having a gun, so I have to be brave and put up with it. I don't know what else to do.' We clung to each other for a minute and she gave me a dry little kiss on the cheek (her lips were always dry now) then pulled herself together and said she'd like a brandy and dry before dinner.

She decided that she wanted to walk again, and every time we visited, she asked us to help her practise with her walking frame. We held her arm as she took some small, limping steps down the corridor for a few minutes and then became tired and had to stop. We knew she would never be able to walk independently again, because of her shakiness and poor eyesight and confusion, but we did not tell her. We just watched her practise with grim determination.

One afternoon I found her in the lounge-room with some of the other residents. Most of them were in wheel-chairs but she was in a day-bed which was more comfortable after her hip operation. She was wearing bright clothes and lipstick and her blue eyes darted around the room. Outside the window it was grey and raining lightly.

'It's good to see you out of bed,' I said, sitting beside her.

'They're having a church service and I asked to be brought up here,' she said, and I wondered if she was bored or seeking the solace of religion now that she was nearing the end of her life. She was brought up a strict Presbyterian, but as far as I knew she had not been to a church service for over forty years, apart from weddings and funerals. The minister came in, carrying a purple scarf and a small silver container. He wore a grey suit and dog collar and smiled a lot.

'What sort of minister is he?' I whispered to Mum.

'C of E,' she whispered back.

The minister looked around and smiled. 'Thank you all for joining us today,' he said and placed the silver bowl on the table. He put the purple cloth around his neck and opened with a prayer. Most of the ladies closed their eyes and I glanced at Mum and saw that hers were shut too. The prayer finished and everyone opened their eyes except Mum. Perhaps she was resting.

The minister read from the Bible, *'Blessed are the poor in spirit . . . blessed are the peacemakers.'* I remembered that passage from my childhood. Mum's head fell lower on her chest and she dozed. The minister spoke and smiled some more and then intoned the Lord's Prayer. Some of the residents said it with him, but others were dozing now too. I had a flashback to my schooldays when I stopped saying the Lord's Prayer when I decided I was no longer a believer. I remembered how difficult it was being the outsider while everyone else mumbled away.

When the prayer was finished, the minister spoke about confessing. *'We have all sinned,'* he said, *'and God sits in judgement on us. We must confess our sins and we will be forgiven.'* I wondered what kind of sins these dear old ladies could be committing. Some were deaf, some were blind, and all were frail and slept a lot. It didn't leave much room for vice. But now he was talking about God being all-merciful, which seemed a bit contradictory with the judgement business. The ladies were listening carefully – those who were not asleep – and I could see that they found this service comforting, and that he was a kindly, gentle minister.

Mum was still dozing. The minister said he would now administer the Blessed Sacrament. Mum lifted her head and opened her eyes. I had never seen this ritual and guessed she hadn't either. The minister spoke about Jesus being the Lamb of God and how we would now eat the flesh and drink the blood. It seemed rather cannibalistic. He opened the silver container and held it in one hand while he approached the nearest old lady, and asked if she would like to take the sacrament. She nodded her head in agreement and he took out a tiny circular wafer of bread. He placed it on her tongue and intoned gently before moving on to the next person.

I watched him go round the circle. Everyone took the sacrament. Finally he got to us and hesitated. He turned to me and said, 'Would this lady like to take the sacrament?'

'I think you'd better ask her.'

He bent towards Mum and said, 'Do you normally take the sacrament?'

'Not recently,' she said.

'Would you like to now?'

Mum said 'all right,' and he popped the wafer on her tongue, intoned and moved on. When his back was turned and no-one was looking, she took it out of her mouth and gave it to me and whispered, 'Take it away.'

'You're meant to swallow it,' I whispered back.

'No thanks, it has no taste.'

I took the damp wafer and put it in my pocket. The minister had now finished the service and was going around the circle again making conversation. He bent over each old lady and took her hand and asked politely how she was. 'Not very well,' said one in a little voice. Another one said, 'Thank you so much for the service,' with her eyes shining. When he came to us, I said, 'This is my mother, her name is Eileen, she's new here.'

'Hello Eileen,' he said.

'Hello,' she said, 'did you get wet coming here?'

He glanced out the window at the rain and said, 'No, I had my car.' The other ladies stared. Good for her, I thought, she's still got life in her and she's not too confused today. She had forgotten how to smile, but perhaps that would return.

When the minister left, there was an hour free before dinner and I put on a CD of my sister singing. It was happy music with a good beat. Most of the ladies dropped their heads and went to sleep. 'They can't hear it,' said Mum, 'they're mostly deaf,' but I left it on and when a nurse came in and heard the beat, she smiled and danced a few steps around the room. Then she poured wine or apple juice for those around the table and gave me a broad smile as I poured Mum a brandy and dry ginger.

I was full of admiration for the staff in this nursing home, for their patience and kindness and good humour. I thought of the saying that the elderly make a gift to us, by giving us the opportunity to show compassion. I asked my mother if she was getting a bit happier. 'Not happy,' she said, 'but perhaps a bit more resigned. Yes, that's the word, resigned.'

Shortly before Christmas my brother and I sat in a café and discussed Mum's situation. 'Lorraine and I have decided to stay in Melbourne as long as she's alive,' my brother said, 'no matter how long it takes. We won't leave you to do it alone anymore.' I was deeply grateful, but surprised. Melbourne was no longer their home. They were only here because of Mum, and had been staying with friends for the past three months.

'What about the boat?' I asked. Their home was a yacht they had been living on for eight years. It was currently moored in Barcelona. My brother had retired in his fifties and embarked on his life-long dream of sailing around the world. He and Lorraine had sold their house in Melbourne, purchased a yacht and sailed slowly from Australia to Thailand. They had stayed in Phuket for a year then sailed up through the Red Sea to Turkey. After a year there, exploring the Eastern Mediterranean, they moved on to Barcelona. They had planned to sail across to South America when Mum became ill.

'We'll sell it,' he said. 'We wouldn't feel right if we left you now.'

I was shocked. 'Can't you just leave it with friends until you see what happens with Mum?'

'No, we can't do that. You need to do a couple of hours' maintenance on it every day and we can't rely on others to do that. We'll need to do a lot of work on it just to get it ready to sell.'

I hugged my brother with affection and reflected that one good thing had come out of my mother's illness. It had brought us closer together – my brother, his partner, my sister and me. When my brother was with Mum, he showed a gentle, caring side that I had hardly seen before. He was a man of action, and in the nursing home there was little he could do. He brought her chocolates, avocado and mangoes, put moisturiser on her dry skin, wheeled her around and talked to the nurses and residents. One day I even found him with a small toolkit, pumping up all the wheelchairs. I sighed at the thought that this could go on for years.

'You look tired,' he said. 'Lorraine and I want you to take all of January off and we'll look after Mum. Later on you can return the favour, because we'll have to go back to Barcelona and fix up the boat ready to sell it.' A whole month off! I felt tears come to my eyes and thanked him. All I could think of was getting through Christmas and then stopping. I just wanted to rest and read and not see anybody except Race and the family, until I recovered.

16

Bindara

'I had just turned sixty, but I felt more at peace than ever before . . . and was doing what I had long wanted to do, writing and reflecting.'

Sometime after Christmas, I met a friend my age whose older husband had Alzheimer's. He lived in a cottage they owned in the country, and had a number of carers coming in to help. His wife and daughter went up and down from Melbourne to visit, but did not live with him all the time. 'He's quite happy,' my friend said, 'he has our two dogs and people to talk to and he reads a lot. He understands what he reads, but forgets it quickly. He can read a book and then read it again three weeks later.'

This woman was a successful artist and told me she had won a scholarship to go to Italy for a few months to paint. She looked embarrassed and then blurted out, 'I decided to continue with my own life. I'm just not cut out for looking after him all the time.' She was a warm and caring person and I wondered what inner struggle she had gone through before reaching that decision. I admired her self-preservation, and wondered what I would do in her situation. Then I thought about my mother, who was making me feel guilty because I was taking January 'off.' I needed some self-preservation too.

It reminded me of when our children were small, and my friends and I had to make difficult decisions about when to go back to work, and when to switch from part-time to full-time work. We were part of the pioneering generation of feminists who chose to have a career as well as a family. Now our children were grown up, we were combining our work with looking after elderly parents and grandchildren, or in my friend's case, an ailing husband. Then and now, we had to made sure our own needs were not swallowed up. After the horrors of the past few months with my mother, I needed some time for myself.

So in mid-January when most people migrated to the beach, I went to the country to write and to think. I stayed at Bindara, a farm and a kind of animal sanctuary north of Melbourne, in rolling hills. I'd heard about it from a friend who stayed there while writing a book about philosophy and ecology. 'The little studio is neat, pretty and clean,' she said. 'It's away from the house and you won't be disturbed.'

The studio was built of stone and was large and full of light. French windows opened onto a small courtyard covered with wisteria. I had expected the furnishings to be basic, or perhaps overly-fussy in the usual bed and breakfast style. Instead, there were Persian rugs on the floor, solid oak furniture, some good lamps and pottery and large paintings of the Australian bush. The studio had a bed-sitting room with a small kitchen and bathroom attached. It was the perfect treat.

When I arrived it was over thirty degrees Celsius and the doors of the studio were open to catch the tiny breeze. I changed into shorts and a t-shirt and went out to explore the farm. Everywhere the drought was present, in the dry, bone-coloured grass, the listless plants and trees and the haze on the hills from distant bushfires. The newspapers said it was the worst drought in Australia in a hundred years. Everything was still, in the hot heaviness of the Australian bush.

Below the studio I found an empty creek bed and followed the path beside it through stringy gum trees, rockeries and wilting plants. On the hill above, a kangaroo suddenly bounded through the bush and then all was silent again. In a half-empty fishpond, an echidna drank from the murky sludge at the bottom. I climbed up the path, past a small bridge and into a formal garden in front of the main house. A goose wandered about, honking. A silky grey dog came out of the house and licked my hand. Further on, I came to a small lake which was now just a gaping wound, its cracked surface baking in the sun.

I tracked back through the rose garden and stone statues beside the parched lawns, and walked up onto a rise. There I found a white wrought-iron seat which looked out towards the hills. Everything was silent, except for the flies buzzing in the heat, the chirp of small birds, and the caw-caw of crows and cockatoos. I looked across the pale, undulating fields, sprinkled with stone boulders formed by the lava of a volcano millions of years earlier.

I thought of the early settlers and their back-breaking work clearing the trees and the great lumps of granite. How frightened they were in this bush, by the topsy-turvy seasons, the snakes and spiders and the strange animals and plants. It was so different from all they knew, whereas those of us born here love its harsh beauty. I sat for a while enjoying the silence, the open space and the light.

Further along the driveway I found Peter, the owner, fixing a hose near a large shed. My friend had told me that he was a gentle man who loved animals, and he showed me his ostriches and donkeys. In a paddock near the shed he pointed out Alpacas, which looked like a cross between a lamb and a giraffe, and in another paddock some long-horned highland cattle. Near them were Suffolk sheep with small black faces. Peter told me they spent most of their time in the shed, where there was an old black and white television. I liked his laconic Aussie humour.

The animals were his pets, he explained, and he fed them by hand twice a day. He was once a gardener in the city and had created this sanctuary by himself, but now he was worn down by the drought which had destroyed so much of his garden and closed his nursery. 'It hasn't rained properly for months,' he said, 'We had some light rain in winter, but no run-off for the dams. The problem goes back much longer than that though. The creek hasn't run for years now. Even the trees in the hills are stressed, and the koalas died out long ago.'

He said he had to buy water and hay for the animals, which was very expensive. He also kept a water-hole filled for the kangaroos and other wild animals. We talked about the bushfires which were dotted all over the state, and Peter said if he caught one of the people who started the fires, he would shoot them. 'They cause such suffering for the animals,' he said. 'Humans are all right, they can get away, they can look after themselves, but the animals can't.'

I continued my walk up the long driveway and the only sound was the crunch of my shoes on the gravel. I stopped and felt the silence and the wide spaces. In the paddocks, the dams were covered with only a few inches of muddy water or were empty, like brown scabs.

It took me about twenty minutes to reach the road. Then I turned and walked back along the driveway to the shed. The largest ostrich, taller than a man, ran to the wire fence to meet me. We stared at each other. Then it knelt down in the dirt and spread its massive wings, bared its greyish-pink flanks obscenely and did a strange dance, beating its head from side to side against its wings – bang, bang, bang. I found Peter and asked what this meant. Was it trying to get some cool air under its wings?

Peter laughed. 'No, it thinks you're a good sort.'

'What?'

'It's the mating season. It's in love with you!'

As I laughed, he warned me not to get too close to the ostrich. 'It can be very stroppy,' he said. 'It bailed me up the other day and wouldn't let me go into the shed.'

After lunch I sat on my little veranda, looking out. I melted into the world around me and felt as though I could sit there forever. It was bliss to let my mind roam wherever it liked, uninterrupted. I'd escaped from all my responsibilities, including my mother. My brother had told her I was away and could not be contacted and I was happy to keep it that way. I watched a male peacock step onto the veranda and wander across, trailing its brilliant blue and green feathers. He was followed by a silky bantam hen, white and fluffy as a French poodle. Her brown and white chicks followed, their little heads bobbing as they poked inquisitively under the deck chairs and into the pot-plants.

I thought about why I was at Bindara – to work my way back into the novel I was trying to write about my long-ago love affair in Paris. To wrestle with another, smaller, block against writing. What was this story for? Where was it going? Five months earlier I thought I knew, but then my mother became ill and everything changed. For months now I had done nothing but look after her, in hospitals and nursing homes. There had been no time to write, and I seemed to have lost interest in this novel or memoir or whatever it was going to be, and I wondered why. How can you write over 30,000 words and then lose interest? You're almost half way towards a book. I thought of a writer who once said, 'Beware the pause that lasts too long.'

I thought I knew why I'd lost interest. Much of the motivation for writing about that period in my life was the need to live it again, to understand it better and to heal some wounds from the past. To a certain extent, the writing had done that already. Could it be that the 'therapy' had worked? The writing had certainly shifted my perspective on much of what had taken place all those years ago. Or could it be that I was running away from the end of the story, with its pain and feelings of betrayal? After five months absence from writing, I'd lost touch with the world I was trying to create. But the story was only half told and I needed to take it to the end and finish it, and then be done with it.

Later that day, I explored some paths near the studio, which led to more animal enclosures and the plant nursery. I found Peter making a water container for the goannas. He told me he'd set traps for foxes, because they were trying to get the baby peacocks. Behind the shed in which he was working, I saw a wallaby and some emus.

I wandered up the path to a low, corrugated-iron enclosure, where ferrets slept in the sun, curled around each other in glossy gold and brown balls of fur. A young ferret, bored with napping, ran through large curved pipes set up for his play. In another enclosure, pheasants pecked at the ground and a kookaburra looked down on them from its perch and then broke into its strange laugh. There were brilliant Rosellas, guinea hens and a pig so large its spindly legs could hardly hold it up. I passed wombats, ducks, geese, tame kangaroos and exotic poultry.

As I returned to the main driveway, I came upon the male peacock in full display, its brilliant feathers spread in an arc, gently fanning back and forth. As I watched, he slowly turned in a circle while his rear feathers, brown and speckled grey, quivered passionately. It was another mating ritual in this overheated landscape. A female pea-hen, drably brown, wandered by and pecked at the ground. She ignored the male and disappeared into the bushes. The male continued to display himself, his head held high, with its small crown on top. Then he turned away gracefully, swept his feathers closed behind him and leaped onto a piece of rusted farm machinery on the side of the path. He stood there haughtily, his tail sweeping the ground.

That evening, I found some compact disks in a

cupboard and played a selection. I cooked a simple meal of steak and salad while Handel's Largo washed through the room. After dinner, I sat on the veranda eating fresh peaches, while the birds flew round in a frenzy as night closed in.

The next day I sat working at the dining table, listening to the wind in the trees, the birds, and the shrill cry of the peacocks. I spent the first two days reading the book from start to finish for the first time since I'd started writing it. I made notes as I went, as ideas occurred for improving each section. Why did some characters appear and never appear again? Would it be better in the first person or the third person? And again, the vexed question that had haunted me all along – was it to be a novel or a memoir?

The idea of memoir still made me afraid. I had not thought about the story for months and the seeds of doubt had multiplied on the empty ground. My main fear was still the same, how could I expose myself so much, even though the events had taken place thirty-five years earlier and were now camouflaged by fiction? How could I write about people who were still alive, who might read it and take offence?

Every Christmas for over thirty years, I'd exchanged a brief letter with my former lover. This year I had told him that I was now a grandmother, and that I was writing a book, but I didn't tell him what it was about. He replied immediately, saying he wanted to read it. He went on to say that he was now eighty and had just had triple bypass heart surgery. 'Only your Christmas messages keep me alive,' he wrote and added, 'If I die, my wife will let you know.' All this confused me further. Did I want to show it to him? What if he died, did I want to show it to his family? His wife was also unwell. How would they feel about what I'd written?

I thought about the brief letters we'd exchanged over the years, and wondered what it meant. Who now were these people I had not seen in decades and who were frozen in my memory as they were thirty-five years earlier? He had told me in his Christmas letter that his second daughter was now a well-known artist and that I should look up her website. When I did, I was stunned by her talent, but even more so by her photograph. It showed a beautiful woman in her forties with dark hair and an uncanny resemblance to her mother as she was when I knew her.

I stared at the photo for a long time, shocked into the realization that I was living with ghosts. My mind was full of the images of people as they were when I last saw them. Now they were old, but I did not know them as they were now, I only knew them as they were then.

Well, said my inner critic, what's the point of all this wallowing in the past, this *recherche du temps perdu*. I thought of a book discussion I'd heard on the radio, where the announcer declared disdainfully that all first novels were narcissistic. I tried to think of a rebuttal. 'Well,' I said to the announcer, 'most writers write about what they know, which is how they make it real. Proust wrote endlessly about himself – narcissistically if you like – and he created one of the greatest novels of the twentieth century.' Did Proust write from self-love? I thought not. I thought he did it from the same motives as most writers

– to re-create the past, to understand it and to share it. Like most writers, he was full of doubts about his work.

I thought of Somerset Maugham's story about Proust, which was in the preface to a book I was reading. Proust, said Maugham, wanted a certain French magazine to publish an article on his work, and thinking that no-one could write the review as well as he could, sat down and wrote it himself. Proust then asked a young friend of his to put his name to the review and take it to the editor. The young man did so, but after a while the editor said to him, 'I must refuse your article, Marcel Proust would never forgive me if I printed a criticism of his work that was so perfunctory and so unsympathetic.'

Authors always aim for perfection, Maugham said, and feel wretchedly aware that they have not attained it. When I read this it cheered me up considerably, because it expressed so exactly my struggle – the constant search for the right words, for the Holy Grail of perfection, always out of reach. I assumed it was the same for everyone engaged in the creative process. I thought of Monet, getting up before dawn each morning to paint his beloved river at Giverny, trying to capture the light day after day, never satisfied. I thought of a young Australian writer I'd heard at a writer's festival who said, 'You want to create the Taj Mahal, but in the end you think that all you've created is an outdoor dunny.'

Later in the day I left the studio and climbed the hill opposite, up into the trees, through bracken and dry grass. When I was nearly at the top, I sat in a clearing to get a wider view. The trees were so dry that they had shed bark, sticks and boughs which littered the ground like discarded clothes. In some places an entire tree had hollowed out and fallen to the ground, lifeless.

I wiped the sweat from my forehead and let the silence seep into me. Up there I had a clear view of the hills and valleys for miles around. I saw the occasional clutch of cypresses or pine trees around a red-roofed farmhouse. Everything was still and silent. After a while I sensed the timelessness of the land. Those dry hills and stones had been there, immobile, for eons. What did they care about our petty struggles and passions?

I thought of a book that had recently touched me, *The Same Sea*, by the Israeli writer Amos Oz. It was a story about age and youth and yearning. The author was in his early sixties and he entered the book at times, inserting himself into the action. You sensed a man facing up to his own mortality, his soul searching for rest. He thought of the eternal nature of the mountains and the sea and there was sadness in his reflections. But then he told us he lost his mother when he was a child, and I wondered if this explained his melancholy. The wound that would not heal. I knew a lot about that wound because I had three step-children who lost their mother when they were young. They were adults now, with children of their own, but the scars remained.

And besides, I thought, Amos Oz had other reasons to be sad. Who would not be, living in Israel and being a campaigner for peace? Who could not feel depressed, watching powerlessly while the leaders of Israel and Palestine played out the dance of death, the only dance they knew. I didn't want Amos Oz to be sad. I wanted to tell him that Life was good. I too was facing my own mortality, but it didn't frighten me. I had just turned sixty, but I felt more at peace than ever before. I had left the world of work behind, with its stresses and responsibilities, and was doing what I had long wanted to do, writing and reflecting.

Back in the studio, my thoughts turn to Somerset Maugham, who also lost his mother when he was a child. I was re-reading *Of Human Bondage*, a novel based on Maugham's childhood, his time as a medical student and his decision to become a writer. I turned to the preface, where Maugham explained that he wrote a similar story when he was twenty-three, but could not find a publisher. That was a good thing, he said, because we need distance in order to understand the past. He became a distinguished playwright, but at the age of thirty-seven, the memories of his past persisted so strongly and painfully that he had to stop and write about it, in order to free himself. He wrote the book non-stop in two years, and it did free him.

'*Of Human Bondage*,' he wrote, '*is not an autobiography, but an autobiographical novel; fact and fiction are inextricably mingled; the emotions are my own, but not all the incidents are related as they happened, and some of them are transferred to my hero not from my own life but from that of persons with whom I was intimate.*' I felt encouraged by those words. That was what I was trying to do with my own story, to free myself from the past and to mingle fact and fiction.

The next day I finished reading everything I had written and felt it was both better and worse than I'd hoped. I saw flaws everywhere, but there were one or two passages which moved me, and perhaps might move someone else. As I was drawn back into the story, I realized that I did in fact want to continue it. I wanted to see what would happen, because it had become more than memory now, it had developed a life of its own.

I opened my laptop and tried to write the next chapter, but I was stuck. I wasn't ready. I pushed the laptop away and re-read some of my diaries of that long-ago time in Paris, and the letters home to my parents, which they had kept faithfully for me. I tried to think myself back into the mind of my twenty-five year old self.

I looked out the window, marvelling at how much I was enjoying the solitude. I thought of Dorothea Brande's book *Becoming a Writer*, in which she said writers thrive best on solitude, on a simple routine with occasional time off for fun. Spend your time in silent recreations, she said, like walking, listening to music or knitting. While you're doing these things, think about what you want to write and daydream about it. Avoid conversations and other activities which will distract you.

In my Paris diaries, I saw that even in my twenties I loved writing and solitude. In those days I was reading the memoirs of Simone de Beauvoir, and I copied into my diary a passage of hers on solitude which moved me. It was from *Force of Circumstance*, when she was on a holiday alone in Tangiers. '*After years of living with others,*' she wrote, '*this encounter with myself stirred me so deeply that I believed it to be the dawn of a sort of wisdom. It was only an interim, but for a long time I kept the palm trees, the sands, and their silence in my heart.*'

I closed the diaries and tried to concentrate on what to

write. My novel had reached the point where the streets of Paris were overtaken by the mini-revolution of 1968. Student riots triggered a nation-wide strike that paralysed the country for weeks and almost brought down the government of General De Gaulle. A new question plagued me. Did I want to write about how I felt at the time, as the upheaval in the streets mirrored the upheaval in my private life, or did I want to invent something new?

All sorts of possibilities entered my mind – my heroine might get injured in the riots, she could fall in love with a student leader or she could break off with her lover because of his attitude to the demonstrations. None of those things happened, but they might have. I could let the story go in a new direction altogether.

I puzzled over this for hours, trying out scenes in my head as I walked around the farm or sat on the veranda. Finally I decided that I would continue as I had so far. I would stay with the emotions of the time, but allow new events to unroll if they suited the story better. I would make my heroine more adventurous and see what happened if she got caught up in the violence of the riots. This was the fun of writing fiction; you could use your imagination and invent whatever you liked.

While I was out walking, I bumped into Peter who said, 'Is the book finished?'

I laughed. 'These things take a long time, years usually.'

He looked puzzled. 'What's it about then? Is it a best seller?'

'Oh, no.' I tried to explain. 'It's about a love affair in Paris a long time ago, and about a revolution and growing up.' I fumbled for words. Ah, the difficulty of explaining to someone else what I was writing, especially when I was only half way there. I had a picture in my head of the shape of the book, but it might turn out to be quite different by the time I finished. He listened patiently.

'Writing a book is like your gardening,' I said. 'You do one bit at a time, slowly, and you create it as you go along.' He nodded his head. Now he understood.

Towards the end of the week, I finally started the next chapter. It started sluggishly, but then it gained momentum and went well for several hours until it stalled at the end of the day. I gave up then and made some pasta, listening to Mozart's Clarinet Concerto, and told myself I'd try again tomorrow.

The next day, after breakfast and a long walk, the story started flowing again, slowly but steadily. When it was time to pack up and leave, I felt I was right back into it. I would be able to continue now, as long as I didn't let too much of a gap come between me and the writing. As long as my mother did not take up all my time. The little studio and the silence had worked their magic and I felt rested and at peace again. As I drove away I made a silent promise: *I will be back.*

17

Glenfern

'I started to think about a room outside the house.
Somewhere I could go each day like a regular job, a place
with no phone and no interruptions.'

Virginia Woolf said it in a famous essay in 1928 – a
writer must have 'A room of one's own.' Back home
after my return from Bindara, I started thinking about
this. My mother had settled into the nursing home and
I had some free time again, but my writing was not going
well.

I had a perfectly good desk at home, in fact two, but
I was finding it hard to write there. Home was a two-
bedroom 'town house' near the city, where Race and I
moved after he retired from politics and the children left
home. At the back of the house we built a light-filled
study which opened onto a small courtyard garden. It was
a big room with two desks, but as Race used it as an office,
I only used my desk there for paying bills or sewing, and
the grandchildren sometimes used it for drawing.

When I started writing again, I put a desk in the second
bedroom. This was the room where children, grand-

children and guests stayed, and after Caleb was born I squeezed a cot in between my desk and the wall, so that he could sometimes stay overnight. I loved this room, which got the morning sun and looked down on the garden of the house next door and trees beyond. I could shut the door and block out the world and when I looked at the cot I thought of Caleb and smiled. I pictured him sleeping there, warm and pink, clutching the cloth nappy which was his 'loved object,' or standing up and holding the bars of the cot, calling out to be picked up. I enjoyed writing in that room, but in your own home there are too many distractions.

When I was younger and my children were small, working from home was not a problem. I was a journalist, driven by deadlines, and worked feverishly because my writing time was limited to the hours when the children were at school and kindergarten. As soon as I dropped them off in the morning I made some coffee, put on a load of washing, went into my study and closed the door. I did not allow myself to emerge other than to get a cup of coffee or to make lunch. Often I had to write an entire article between nine a.m. and three p.m. It concentrated the mind wonderfully.

Now that I was retired however, I was no longer driven by deadlines or the need to earn money, since I had my superannuation. I liked this quiet and more reflective life. Mornings were for writing and afternoons were for other activities such as visiting my mother, minding grand-children or seeing friends. The perfect balance, you might think. But it was too easy for the mornings to disappear into that Bermuda Triangle familiar to all writers.

On a typical morning I would sit at my desk at nine a.m. and check my emails. Some were chatty ones from friends and called for a reply. There's something about emails that makes writing easy – the 'censor' is missing and you burble on. An hour would go by. Then the phone would ring and I'd get involved in a discussion with Race about some domestic matter and another half hour would be gone.

I'd return to my desk and file my nails while I thought about what to write. Time would slip away. Then it would be time for a cup of tea and while I was waiting for the kettle to boil, I'd water some plants and put on the washing. If I was stopping for tea, then I might read the newspaper too. Afterwards, feeling guilty, I'd return to my desk and say to myself, '*Stop stuffing around.*' I'd make some notes about what I wanted to write and look up a reference book. Then I'd look at my watch. My goodness! Noon already and soon it would be time to have lunch and visit my mother. No use trying to start writing now, I'd make a fresh start tomorrow. I really, really would.

I started to think about a room outside the house. Somewhere I could go each day like a regular job, a place with no phone and no interruptions. *A room of one's own.* I hoped it would lead to better writing, but there was another reason, too. If I left home each morning and returned later in the day, the week would become structured again and the weekends more precious.

When you work from home, every day becomes the same and the weekends disappear. I wanted to relish the weekends again, to keep them free of writing and to look forward to reading the papers in bed when I woke on

Saturday morning. After a life-time of work habits, it had seemed liberating at first to throw those habits away, but now I was beginning to think that some were desirable after all, if only to make you appreciate better the hours when you were not at 'work.'

One morning as I walked along the river, thinking about where to find such a room, I looked up at the graceful curves of Como Park and wondered about 'Como,' the large National Trust house on the hill above. This historic house and garden were open to the public. Perhaps they had a small room tucked away which was not used? I rushed home and phoned them. I explained what I was looking for and said that if they had a room, maybe in exchange I could help with writing, research or public relations. A nice man said he'd like to help, but they were terribly short of space and didn't have enough room for their own activities.

'Do you think there are any other Trust properties which might have a room?' I asked.

'Well as a matter of fact, there might be,' he said. 'We have a property called Glenfern in Hotham Street, East St Kilda, on the corner of Inkerman Street. There might be something there.' My heart lifted. I knew the area well – it was only ten minutes' drive from my house. The corner he mentioned was one of the main Jewish areas of Melbourne. There was a Jewish school and synagogue there, and on Saturdays you could see Orthodox men and boys walking past in black coats and hats, some with beards and ringlets, the women in wigs and sombre clothes.

In the shopping centre nearby, the cafes served schnitzel and goulash and the delicatessens sold matzo balls, gefilte fish and blintzes. The area was rich and exotic, humming with voices in many different languages. I drove down this road almost every day, but had never heard of Glenfern.

'You should ring Richard Heathcote, the Trust's Development Officer,' he said, and gave me a phone number. Feeling excited, I phoned Richard Heathcote, who was very helpful and friendly. Glenfern, he said, was once owned by the Boyd family, and was given to the Trust by a subsequent owner, Miss Ostberg. Next to the house was a block of flats which were built by Miss Ostberg to obtain revenue for the upkeep of the house. Glenfern was only partly renovated, he said, and was not suitable to be opened to the public.

'We have some pianists in residence at Glenfern,' he said, 'and we're thinking of having other artists in residence there, so you and I should have a chat and I'll show you around.'

We arranged to meet in a few days, but I couldn't wait that long and drove straight down to Glenfern. The house was hidden behind a high fence and tall trees. I parked the car and peered through the wrought-iron gates at the front and the side. There was a circular driveway in front of the house and some large, old trees – liquid ambers, eucalyptus and cedars. The house was a two-storey Victorian Gothic villa with steeply pitched slate roofs and a front veranda. It was painted in heritage colours – the stonework a light grey and the trims dark red.

I walked round the back and entered an open car park. The rear of the house was un-renovated, with peeling paint and some crumbling outhouses, old stables and clothes lines. Glenfern was like an old lady who has been to the hairdresser and put on make-up, but on closer inspection turns out to be wrinkled and stooped.

I drove away happily, imagining myself installed in one of the rooms upstairs, looking down onto the front garden. The room would be large and full of cobwebs, but I'd clean it and furnish it and from time to time, run downstairs and stroll in the garden. All this was going to be wonderful and it was really close to home.

I counted the days until I met Richard. He was a tall Englishman with a cheerful manner. 'I'll show you round,' he said, producing a large bunch of keys and unlocking the front door. The house was dark and silent, with brownish-coloured wallpaper and carpet. We entered a large reception room which ran from the front of the house to the back. It was furnished in heritage style and had a grand piano and some plastic seats in rows. 'This room was decorated for the film *Ned Kelly*,' Richard said. 'The pianists use it to practise in, and sometimes hold concerts here and in other Trust houses.'

'Will they be noisy?' I asked anxiously.

'Oh no, I don't think you'll hear them from your room.'

I wondered where my room was and followed him into the hallway. We went up the stairs and he showed me into the top rooms which looked over the garden. There were holes in the ceiling and the plaster was crumbling. These rooms were apparently not where I would be, because we moved on to the back of the house which was even more run-down. Every time we approached a door, Richard had to find a key and unlock it. He waved the bunch of keys at me and said with a grin, 'Welcome to the world of Trust property management.'

He led the way through a rabbit-warren of small rooms, filled with furniture covered in dust-cloths and boxes of different sizes. Everything had a closed-up, musty smell. A packet of rat poison sat in the corner of each room. He explained that this back part was converted by Miss Ostberg into small flats which she rented out. I was beginning to think of her as Miss Haversham.

Eventually we found ourselves in a passage on the ground floor at the back of the house. This led into a small room filled with Trust materials. Richard opened some dusty Venetian blinds and I saw that we were facing the brick flats, just a few feet away. A door led outside, but Richard couldn't find the key. He opened another door into an even smaller room, also crammed with Trust materials. The room was dark and airless. He turned on the light.

'Well, this is it,' he said breezily, 'what do you think?' He looked at me expectantly, but I found the place depressing and couldn't think of anything to say.

'We'll remove everything and provide you with some paint to fix it up,' he said quickly. 'You can have your own key and come and go as you please, from the door that leads outside.' I look around, trying to imagine how it might be improved. The plaster was peeling, the carpet was worn and striped, and the walls were grey. The worst thing was that the room faced south and would never have any direct sun, and the flats outside with their brick walls and straggling pot plants were a far cry from the garden view I'd dreamed of.

'I don't suppose there's a room facing the front?' I murmured, and he said no, they were not available. He was waiting for my response, so I said, 'It's interesting,' and asked if I could have a couple of days to think about it. He agreed. I asked if there was a toilet and he showed me a bathroom off one of the corridors. It was old but clean.

We retraced our steps, locking doors as we went, and ended up outside my little room, next to the flats. There was a small porch over the doorway, covered with broken lattice-work. Everything on this side of the old house seemed neglected and unloved. There were gutters which hung drunkenly, cracked window panes and a rickety staircase to the second floor.

'All it needs is a climbing rose over the porch and it would be quite romantic,' I said jokingly. Richard grinned. We went round to the front garden and sat on a bench and he told me about the house.

'Glenfern was built in 1857 and the Boyd family owned it from 1876 to 1901,' he began. I nodded. The family was well known – Arthur Boyd was one of Australia's most famous artists and there were several generations of Boyds and their relatives who were artists, sculptors, writers and architects.

'Later on the Ostberg family owned it,' he said, 'and the last member of that family, Miss Amy Ostberg, left it to the Trust when she died in 1984. The property has been quite a problem for us – we can't sell any of it or use it for anything other than Trust business. The rent from the flats is used for renovations, but that's a slow process. So far we've only done basic things like repairing the roof and painting the front part. In a year or two we may have enough to fix up the East wing, where your room is, and that's where we might have a number of writers or artists-in-residence. If you take the room, perhaps you could help us develop the concept for how that might work.'

It seemed a wonderful coincidence that they were thinking of rooms for writers. I told Richard there were writers' retreats in other parts of Australia, but none in our state of Victoria, so the idea should gain support. I was happy to help develop the concept, but I was worried about the room. Did I really want it? Suddenly my little room at home seemed infinitely preferable.

When I got home, I consulted the family. Talya said, 'Beggars can't be choosers, can they?' She was right. If I turned this down I'd never know if it would have worked. I phoned Richard a few days later and told him I'd take the room.

'Well, well,' he said, 'I was pretty sure you'd say no.'

'It wasn't quite what I expected – I guess it showed.' We laughed.

Weeks went by while we exchanged letters and Richard organized people to clean out the room and make it safe. Eventually I was given a key and some paint. I chose a colour called 'Pale Dogwood' which was off-white with a touch of pink. A friend recommended a painter, a wild looking man with dreadlocks who arrived on a bicycle. He did a good job and was finished in a few hours. I cleaned the windows and the bathroom. The painter ripped up layers of old carpet and I mopped the dark, cracked linoleum underneath.

The room was starting to look better, but it was still

empty and musty. As I was sweeping out the little porch outside my door, an older woman came out of the flat opposite and said hello. 'I'm Feroma,' she said. I asked her to spell it. 'F-r-o-a-m-a. It's Russian, but I come from Ireland. Are you moving in?' I explained what I was doing.

'This section of the house hasn't been lived in for a long time,' she said. 'It's good that you'll be here. Please come in for a cup of coffee any time.' She gave me a broad smile. A few days later, I arrived with two of my grandchildren to drop off some furniture. Froama came out to greet us and said, 'Do come in for a cup of tea.' I thanked her and explained that I was busy at the moment.

That night, I lay awake and worried. Would I be able to write in this little room? It felt cold and soul-less. I half expected to be visited by a mouse or a ghost. And what about the people who lived in the flats? Perhaps they were lonely, and if I made friends with them I'd become involved in their problems and end up sitting in my room worrying about them, instead of being able to write. '*Stop being stupid*,' I told myself, '*the success of this room is not how good it feels, but whether it gives you somewhere to work each day instead of being distracted*.'

I invited my older step-daughter, Jane, to visit and asked her advice on transforming the room. She surveyed it with an expert eye. 'You need some light carpet,' she said, 'and I'll get you some bamboo in pots to put outside the window as a screen. The room is so small that you should have in it only things you really like, so you have a little oasis here that you enjoy.' She knew the neighbourhood well and recommended a cafe nearby. We went to Ikea and chose a chair for the desk, a small armchair to put under the window and some material to make gauze curtains which would screen me from prying eyes without blocking out the light.

I bought a trestle table for a desk and some colourful prints of the Australian artist, Margaret Olley, and I took a favourite print from home, a rosy painting of Notre-Dame and the Quai Saint-Michel by the French Impressionist painter Maximilien Luce. I found a small table, covered it with a cloth, and put it beside the armchair. I looked around my house and picked up things for the little room – a red lacquer tray, an electric kettle, some nice mugs and a large, flowery tin in which I put biscuits, tea and coffee.

Finally I got the *pièce de résistance* – a piece of soft, pale grey carpet which Talya found in a warehouse. When I put it down and arranged the furniture and tacked up the pictures, suddenly everything looked light and pretty. I sat at the desk and looked out the window. The view was not so bad really. Then I walked in the garden and picked some camellias and put them in a vase on the desk. I was happy with my room.

The next time I visited it was a Saturday. It was a lovely sunny day and I opened the window and the porch door to let in fresh air. Somewhere in the flats opposite I could hear music turned down low and the drone of a vacuum cleaner, but I didn't care. I plugged in my laptop and started writing and after a while it began to flow. I hoped that here, in this little room, I would have some moments when it not only flowed, but sparkled. I always knew when it was going well because it stopped being hard work and came alive. At moments like that I felt excited by what I was writing and the words flew onto the page. It didn't happen often, but it was the reward for all the hard slog in between.

While I was working, there was a knock at the door. A man in a dark shirt and jeans stood at the door, smiling. 'Hi, I'm Greg,' he said. 'I live in the flat upstairs with Anne. We just wanted to welcome you.' He told me he had lived at Glenfern for nearly twenty years. I remembered that Richard had told me a woman called Anne lived in a flat upstairs at the front of the house. We chatted for a few minutes and then he left.

A short time later, there was another knock at the door. A woman with soft wavy hair, shorts and a T shirt, smiled at me. 'I'm Anne,' she said. 'Richard wrote to all the people in the flats telling them you were here, as the writer-in-residence. Greg and I are having coffee in the garden – would you like to join us?' I thanked her and showed her the room. 'Oh, I love Margaret Olley,' she said, looking around. 'You'll write a nice novel here.' We smiled at each other.

I locked up and followed her into the garden, surprised by what she'd said. Suddenly I was an official person, the *'Writer-in-Residence.'* It upped the ante somewhat. Now I would have to finish something and try to publish it. A good thing they didn't know what a tenuous hold I had on this novel, and my constant doubts about whether it was any good. A table was set up under the big tree in front of the house, with a pot of coffee, a plate of buttered fruit-loaf and the newspapers. I munched on fruit-loaf while Greg and Anne told me all about Glenfern and its history. Greg said, 'I used to be the caretaker here after Miss Ostberg died. Anne lived in the flat upstairs – I married the girl next door.'

I discovered that Anne was a librarian and Greg was a mechanic and a chauffeur for vintage cars. I asked about the trees, and Greg explained that the one we were sitting under was a deodar cedar and he showed me where the possums had eaten away the tops of the liquid ambers. We were joined by two teenage girls who smiled shyly and exchanged jokes with Greg and Anne. 'They used to live here,' Greg explained, 'in fact the younger one was born here.' They walked away towards the flats. While Greg and Anne filled me in on the Glenfern community, two more residents were introduced and a golden Labrador sniffed around in the bushes.

As I got up to leave they said, 'Join us any time, and use this table if you want to work in the garden. We're a happy crew at Glenfern. You'll enjoy it here.'

I wandered happily through the garden back to my room. I wanted to know more about the Boyds, and decided to read the book about them by the Melbourne writer Brenda Niall. It occurred to me that you didn't have to go to exotic locations in order to find something to write about; there were plenty of interesting subjects close by.

As I sat at my desk again, I thought of Nigel Nicolson, whose memoir 'Long Life' I'd just finished. He was the son of the famous Bloomsbury couple Harold Nicolson and Vita Sackville-West and grew up in Sissinghurst with its famous garden. He had a rich life as a writer, publisher and Member of Parliament, but what sprang to my mind was that in later life, living alone at Sissinghurst, he slowed down and wrote about subjects nearer at hand. He wrote a book on Jane Austen and another on his county, Kent. He was eighty when he wrote his memoirs, but they were fresh, crisp and amusing.

Even closer to home, I thought of a book written by an elderly Australian woman who lived in a nursing home. She called her book, *This Bed My Centre*. I loved the idea that writing was an occupation you could continue no matter where you lived and no matter what your circumstances were, as long as you were still interested in the world around you.

I had recently turned sixty, but I had never felt so much at peace. I had been trying to return to writing since my early fifties and I'd finally made it. I'd gone through the journey described by Peter O'Connor in his book *Facing the Fifties*, and at last had the life I wanted.

O'Connor said the sixties were a time for expanded horizons, for learning new things and for creative endeavours, a time for meeting your own needs and for serving the community. That was certainly true for me. I was now able to combine my writing with being a grandmother and caring for my mother. In addition, I had the exciting new project of transforming Glenfern into a writers' house.

The next day I returned with a copy of *A Room of One's Own*, to find the exact quote from Virginia Woolf. I sat in the armchair and found it on the second page, '*A woman must have money and a room of her own if she is to write fiction.*' I had not read the book for years and wondered why she restricted herself to fiction. I read on and found that it was because she was invited to give a paper on

'Women and Fiction' to two of the women's colleges at Oxford and later turned it into this little book, published in 1928. I read on and couldn't stop. It was so brilliant, so dazzling in fact, that I was carried along with pure pleasure, marvelling at her skill.

At the end of the book she returned to the *'room of one's own'* and said it must have a lock on the door. If you have enough money to support yourself, she said, you have the power to contemplate. If you have a lock on the door, you have the power to think for yourself. 'I hope you will possess yourselves of money enough to travel and to idle,' she told the young women at Oxford, 'to contemplate the future or the past of the world, to dream over books and loiter at street corners and let the line of thought dip deep into the stream, for I am by no means confining you to fiction.'

Praise and blame alike mean nothing, she said, one book will be called both a great book and a worthless book. 'So long as you write what you wish to write, that is all that matters,' she said, and later, 'It is much more important to be oneself than anything else.' I sat back and looked out the window and sighed. That, for me, was the most important message in the book. It was, I thought, the hardest thing for people trying to write. How to go deep inside yourself and find out what wanted to be expressed, regardless of all the 'thou shalts' and 'thou shalt nots' and 'what would others think,' built up over a lifetime. Those barriers, those censors, stood so often in the way of the best writing.

I finished Virginia Woolf's little book with a mixture of ruefulness and happiness. Rueful, because in the presence of such genius it hardly seemed worth trying to write at all, given that the result would always be as insignificant as an ant to a giant. But happy nevertheless, because Virginia Woolf elevated the act of writing to a calling of the highest order:

'When I ask you to write more books I am urging you to do what will be for your good and for the good of the world at large ... What is meant by reality? It would seem to be something very erratic, very undependable – now to be found in a dusty road, now in a scrap of newspaper in the street, now a daffodil in the sun. It lights up a group in a room and stamps some casual saying. It overwhelms one walking home beneath the stars and makes the silent world more real than the world of speech ... Now the writer, as I think, has the chance to live more than other people in the presence of this reality. It is his business to find it and collect it and communicate it to the rest of us. So at least I infer from reading *Lear* or *Emma* or *La Recherche du temps perdu*. For the reading of these books seems to perform a curious couching operation on the senses; one sees more intensely afterwards; the world seems bared of its covering and given an intenser life. So that when I ask you to earn money and have a room of your own, I am asking you to live in the presence of reality, an invigorating life, it would appear, whether one can impart it or not.'

I put down my copy of Virginia Woolf and gazed around the little room again, feeling inspired. I had everything she recommended – a room with a lock on the door; time to dream and to look at the world more intently, and the nice Glenfern community as a bonus. I could hardly believe my luck.

18

Mum's last years

'She had wanted to "fly away" since her stroke four years earlier, and finally her wish was granted.'

When I arrived at Glenfern my mother was ninety-five and trying to resign herself to life in a nursing home. She was confined to a wheelchair and could do little for herself. 'I've lived too long,' she said, 'I've had a wonderful life and I'm ready to go.'

The sad fact is that she limped on to almost a hundred. When I tell people my mother lived to ninety-nine and a half, they gasp and say, 'how lucky you are to have such good genes.' But they're wrong. It's no pleasure to live that long if you're in a nursing home and unwell. My mother's decline in those last years was like someone falling down a cliff strewn with sharp boulders, bumping from one jagged edge to another. From time to time she begged us to end it, but there was little we could do.

At ninety-five she had broken her left hip and had an operation, which is why she was in the wheelchair. Most of the time she was frustrated, but sometimes she showed her old sense of humour. When the carers in the nursing home were showering her one day, she complained of her hip being sore and said it was because it had a screw in it. One of the nurses smiled and said, 'Actually Eileen, you have three screws in it.' My mother said, 'Well three screws are bound to hurt more than one.' The nurse told me later they all broke up laughing and she was sure my mother got this 'naughty' joke.

But mostly she was miserable. As the months went by, she became more and more depressed by her lack of mobility and her failing vision. Her confusion increased and she became mildly paranoid, sometimes believing that she'd been locked up in a dark room. The nurses and carers were wonderful. Their patience, kindness and good humour taught me a lot. They called in a psychogeriatrician who changed her anti-depressants, but things only improved for a while.

My brother and I decided to set boundaries. We visited Mum twice a week and limited our visits to two hours maximum, even though she begged us to stay longer. Each time we left the nursing home we said 'whoopee' at being released, and phoned each other to compare notes.

One day when I was with Mum she said quietly, 'I don't want to go on like this, but I don't know how to end it. I'm ninety-six and everyone says how wonderful it is, but I've had enough. I can't see and I can't *do* anything anymore. They won't let me do *anything* and they get so *cross* with me all the time.'

'I know,' I said, feeling love and pity for her. She was always trying to get out of her wheelchair and the staff and other residents would tell her crossly to sit down, knowing she could fall. She hated being 'ticked off' and her lack of independence and the boredom. Dinner was at a quarter to five and she was then taken back to her room where she could find nothing to do until she was given her sleeping pill at nine pm.

'I don't care if I fall over,' she said one day. 'I don't want to go on any more.'

My brother, his partner Lorraine and I continued our visits, but it was never enough. My sister phoned and sent cards every few days. Sometimes Mum cried and said it was awful being old and at other times she was a prima donna and took out her frustrations on us. When I was with her, she said my brother never came to see her. 'But he was here just a few days ago,' I protested.

'No, he wasn't,' she flashed back, 'he hasn't been to see me in weeks.'

When my brother visited, she said the same thing about me.

A friend of the family visited Mum and said to me, 'It breaks my heart to see her like this. She was always so positive and now she can be quite petulant.' Once when Mum was sick and my brother saw her five times in ten days, I asked him why he visited so often when there was so little pleasure in it. He said, 'so we can live with ourselves.'

Later that year she got out of bed one night, walked to the door and fell, breaking her hip. Her left hip was already held together with screws and pins, and now it was her right one. She was fine during the operation, but went back to the nursing home in a state of confusion from the heavy painkillers. One night they found her crawling down the corridor.

The staff had to watch her constantly. After the evening meal they put her in a day-bed, a kind of tilted chair on wheels, and took her with them while they put everyone else to bed. She hated the daybed, which felt like a prison. She also felt trapped by the special mattress with curved sides which they put on her bed so she could not fall out.

My brother and I went to see her GP and told him that she no longer wanted to 'go on.' He was sympathetic, but said there was little we could do unless she faced a life-threatening illness. Then we could discuss what treatment to give her, or to withhold. 'Once they're in a nursing home,' he said, 'they don't want to go on living, even if they're only eighty-five.'

As he said it, I thought about a book I'd been reading which referred to the nursing home as, '*one of the more doubtful institutions of the twentieth century, developed to cushion and disguise the natural processes of death.*'[1] I thought of a story I'd been told about the Eskimos – that in very old age they put themselves on an iceberg and it floats away.

By the time she was ninety-seven I was having dreams that Mum had died. I woke up feeling happy but guilty.

By ninety-eight she sometimes imagined that terrible things were happening to her. When we told her she was imagining it, she lashed out at us and we learned not to argue back. Her GP said she had advancing dementia and paranoia. He changed her pills and for a while things were better, but then she became depressed and confused again.

By ninety-nine she had ugly blotches on her face which turned out to be skin cancer and we took her to a surgeon to have them removed. Then she lost several front teeth because her jaw was shrinking and there was nothing more a dentist could do. Her legs became stick-like and she developed pressure sores on them. The nurses wrapped her legs in bandages and she wore large lambs-wool slippers like Minnie Mouse.

She lost interest in eating and shrivelled away like a little bird. She slept a lot of the time. On one visit she said to me, 'Please keep coming, it's the only thing worth living for – you bring news from the outside world.' On my next visit she said, 'Have I changed much since I became a little girl?'

By ninety-nine and a half, the nurses finally told us her time had come. The aim now was just to keep her comfortable in bed. A few days before the end I kissed her and told her she was the best Mum ever, but she didn't open her eyes. She was given strong painkillers and a special water mattress to stop bedsores. She developed an infection on her chest and her GP decided, in consultation with us, not to give her antibiotics. He increased her dosage of morphine and she slipped into a coma. In the end she died peacefully. The death certificate said the cause of death was pneumonia and that her last illness was 'general frailty for three years.'

She had wanted to 'fly away' since her stroke four years earlier, and finally her wish was granted. Her death was a release for her and for us. I shed a few tears as I sat by her bed in the last days, but mostly I'd done my grieving for her several years earlier. The woman we knew and loved all our lives had mostly disappeared. I wanted to forget the unhappy, complaining woman of recent years and remember her as she was before.

As I watched her decline, I became more and more convinced that the best course for my mother would have been for her to 'go' when she had her major stroke at ninety-five. Despite having medical power of attorney to refuse treatment, I hadn't been able to bring about the end she wanted. Perhaps if I'd been more vigilant with the doctors when she had the stroke, perhaps if I'd typed up her wishes and hung them on her hospital bed, things might have been different. Perhaps, perhaps. I'll never know, because each case is different and there are no simple answers.

Race and I have discussed this many times and tried to work out how to avoid something similar happening to us when our time comes. As we get older it's an issue that concerns many of our friends as well. Race and I have given each other and our children our medical power of attorney and we've tried to set out our wishes in an 'advance directive.' We are members of 'Dying with Dignity Victoria' (formerly the Voluntary Euthanasia Society of Victoria) and keep up to date with their work and the helpful information they provide.[2]

After my mother died, we had a small 'celebration' of her life, with close family and friends. My brother acted as Master of Ceremonies and then it was my turn to speak.

'As you know,' I said, 'Dad died ten years ago. Some time before that, I had a conversation with him and Mum about funerals. Dad had already arranged all the details for his funeral and prepaid everything. He wanted a large one with a civil celebrant to speak about his c.v. which he'd already prepared. He wanted each of his three children to speak as well. He said he wanted it to be a happy occasion, with a large crowd and plenty of grog. Mum listened to all this with a smile and then said to him, "Why this fuss darling, you won't be there to see it."

'Then I asked her what she wanted for her own funeral. She said, "I want a very, very small gathering with just the immediate family. Make it very brief and then they can all go home. I don't need a speech about what I did." When I raised my eyebrows she giggled and said, "I ran the mother's club and the tuckshop. I married the feller I loved and I had a wonderful life. I did everything I wanted, and that's all you need to say." Then she whispered to me, "Your father's very insecure you know. He wants people to say he was a good chap, and I hope they do."

'This was a classic example of how different Mum and Dad were. He was an introvert, a deep thinker and a worrier. She was a complete extrovert and always happy and positive. They were a great balance for each other.'

I looked up and saw my aunt Dorothy in the front row and we smiled at each other. She was ninety-eight and still fit in mind and body. She and my mother had been very close all their lives and it had hurt her to see my mother's decline.

I turned back to my speech and told them about Mum's childhood. She was born in Rainbow in North-Western Victoria. Her ancestors were Irish and Scottish immigrants. Her father owned the general store and also farmed on a large scale. But there were three years of drought, the farmers couldn't pay the store and the family lost everything. They came to Melbourne for a few years, then returned to the country. Mum and her sister went to boarding school in Melbourne, but when Mum was fifteen her mother became very ill and Mum was sent home to look after her and run the home.

When Mum was twenty, the family moved back to Melbourne to a large home in Hampton with a tennis court and a beach box. Mum always said it was a happy home full of young people playing tennis or swimming, with dancing and card parties at night. In 1938 she married Dad and they started their own family.

'As a child, I remember her always laughing and talking and singing.' I said. 'When I was very small, Carina and I shared a bedroom and Mum used to sing to us before we went to sleep. Our lights would be off and she'd stand at the door, lit by the hall-light, and sing in her lovely clear voice. One of our favourites was called *Cigarette*. It went like this:

> *Cigarette, cigarette*
> *You are warmer and truer*
> *Than any fond wooer, I've met*
> *Cigarette*
> *And it's rapture divine*
> *When your lips are on mine*
> *And I'm kissing my own*
> *Cigarette*

'Mum knew nothing about smoking but she'd pretend to puff on a cigarette and blow smoke rings. She thought smoking was very daring and we giggled. When the song was finished we'd beg for more, and like Nellie Melba, she'd give us a few encores – maybe her theme song, "*Five foot two, eyes of blue, Oh what those five feet could do,"* – before she'd wave and kiss us goodbye and disappear.

'She taught us all to love music, especially jazz. She filled the house with laughter and love and flowers and gave terrific parties. She taught us to do the Charleston on the kitchen floor and taught all our friends to do it too. Even in her nineties she still loved dancing and music. When Dad died and she moved into the retirement home, she still lived a full life, coming and going in her little car to bridge parties or the shops. On weekends she spent the day with Race and me or we took her out to jazz or the theatre. When Kelvin and Lorraine were in Melbourne they took her to restaurants and once or twice a year she flew up to northern NSW to stay with Carina.'

I looked up and told them the story they all knew, about Mum going to a jazz club for her ninety-third birthday and being picked up by a guy with white shoes, and later on how she broke her hip after showing the ladies in the retirement home how to do Greek dancing. Then I reminded them about Mum's starring role as the Queen Mother and celebrating her 100th birthday. She had loved wearing a tiara and putting on a posh accent and making a little speech about the century in which she had lived.

'Shortly after that however,' I said, 'she had a number of falls and operations. She had a kidney removed and a massive stroke. She recovered, but at a diminished level. Her years in the nursing home were full of frustration. She couldn't see well enough to read or watch television; she was confined to a wheelchair and suffered from confusion. She was sometimes in tears and said she wished she had "gone" with the stroke. She tried to be brave and it was very sad to see her in this state.'

'It's time now,' I said, 'to put aside those painful memories and remember her as she really was, so happy and alive. If she could see us all here today she'd say, "don't cry for me; be glad that I had such a long and wonderful life." And she'd laugh and blow us a kiss.'

I looked up and saw people nodding. Yes, that's how they remembered her.

Now it was time for the *pièce de résistance*, a video of Mum's life made by my sister Carina. It was made when Mum was ninety-three and still well, staying in Carina's home in country NSW. The video consisted of photographs of Mum throughout her life, some home movies from the 1940s and 1950s, Mum dancing at my father's eightieth birthday party and Mum playing the Queen mother.

All this was interspersed with footage of Mum in my sister's house, dancing around the kitchen, eating lunch, listening to music, and talking to my sister while looking through the family photo album. It was Mum as we knew her, as alive as though she was in the room with us.

On the soundtrack of the video was my sister's sweet clear voice, singing love songs for Mum – *Five foot two, eyes of blue, – I can't give you anything but love, baby – All of me, why don't you take all of me* – and *Lovin' you, it's easy 'cos you're beautiful.*

As we watched Mum's life unfolding, Carina sang:
I'll be seeing you in all the old familiar places
That this heart of mine embraces, all day through
And then we saw photos of Mum in later life, on

holidays with Dad and with her friends and family. There were more recent photos too. We laughed when we saw her in Phuket, sitting on my brother's yacht, wearing his peaked Captain's cap. In the photo she held up a packet of 'fags' and a can of beer, pretending to be the party girl she was at heart, instead of a woman in her nineties.

I'd seen this video many times but I found it particularly moving now that Mum was gone. My sister had fought with Mum when she was younger, because Mum wanted her to dress in pretty clothes and have ladylike manners, when Carina was a tomboy who wanted to run around in jeans. My sister's struggle to break free went on for a long time, but in later life her anger ceased and she became devoted to Mum. I thought of all this as I listened to my sister's voice, expressing the love we all felt:

If a picture paints a thousand words,
Then why can't I paint you?
The words will never show,
The 'you' I've come to know

We watched photos of Mum and dad with their arms around each other, of Mum kissing her baby grandchildren and of Mum dancing around Carina's kitchen, doing the samba. And as the photos faded out, my sister sang the slow and beautiful last verse:

If the world should stop revolving
Spinning slowly down to die
I'd spend the end with you
When the world was through . . .

Then one by one
The stars would all go out . . .
And you and I
Would sim-pl-y fly a-way.

The screen went blank and we sat in silence for a few moments, hearing the last notes and treasuring the images we had just seen. Then the room broke into laughter and conversation as people turned to each other to share their memories. There were no tears, no funeral dirges. It was just what she would have wanted.

1. Afterword by Jan Carter in *'The illustrated "A Fortunate Life"'* by A.B. Facey. Viking (Penguin) Melbourne 1984.
2. For anyone who wishes to know more about 'refusal of treatment' and 'end of life' decisions, I recommend their website (www.dwdv.org.au) or if you live outside Victoria, any similar organisation.

Epilogue

'There should be a new word for "retirement," to reflect
the fact that most of us can now enjoy twenty or even
thirty years of active and liberated life after we
leave the workplace.'

When I first moved into Glenfern I had a room at the back of the house. I was completely alone there, enjoying the silence. Now, five years later, I have a room upstairs looking down on the garden. As I write, I can hear the doves cooing on a ledge near my window and when I go out into the corridor, I hear the faint sound of Rachmaninoff's second piano concerto being practised in the music room downstairs. The back door bangs and through the window I see one of the other writers cut across the garden to the shops to buy something for lunch.

This is what I dreamed of, a house full of writers who have a quiet retreat but also give each other moral support. We respect each other's privacy, but are comforted by the fact that behind doors other people are typing away or deep in thought. We chat briefly when we meet in the kitchen or the corridor. Once a month we have lunch together and talk about our writing. Friendships are made and there's a useful exchange about deadlines, agents, publishers and the highs and lows of the writing process.

After I moved in, it took several years of planning, fundraising and renovations before the centre was opened. My first job was to do some research on how writers' studios and retreats operated around Australia and overseas. It was fun to read about the New York Public Library which has a special room with cubicles for writers, and Hawthornden Castle in Scotland, where romantic trysts between writers led to some famous marriage break-ups. I invited the Victorian Writers' Centre to be the administrator and we worked with the National Trust of Australia (Vic) to raise the money for the renovations.[2]

We share the house with the 'Team of Pianists' who have been at Glenfern for many years. We have a communal meeting room and kitchen and the use of the large reception rooms at the front of the house for public events. Of the nine studios for writers, two are used by the Australian Poetry Centre and the remaining studios are used by writers for periods of one month to a year. They pay a small rent to cover costs, and some writers have a room rent-free via a fellowship. These fellowships are provided by 'Readings Books and Music' and the Grace Marion Wilson Trust.

So far the studios have been used by writers of fiction, crime fiction, young adult novels, historical novels, film scripts, television scripts, poetry, non-fiction and memoir.

Most of our writers are published or have a contract, and some have won awards. Others are still 'emerging.' The visitor's book tells their stories. One first-time novelist has noted, *'This magical place has taken me on a wonderful journey. I came with one chapter, a file full of historical records, one pen and a journal. Now, three months later, there are eighteen chapters, 50,000 words and the dream that one day this novel will take wings. I will miss the community of writers and the house itself.'*

My own writing has gone on steadily, apart from those periods when my mother was very ill. Two years after arriving at Glenfern I completed my novel set in Paris (140,000 words) and immediately emailed Barbara Turner-Vesselago, the writing teacher whose gave me the kick-start at Queenscliff. She congratulated me and said, *'Finishing a novel is like sailing single-handed around the world.'*

But it was not the end of the novel. There have been two more drafts and it needs another one to shorten it. I'm still not sure whether it should be a novel or memoir. After draft three I put it aside to work on the notes about my mother's decline and my journey towards sixty, which turned into the book you are currently reading.

When I was at Queenscliff, I asked Barbara if it was possible to be a writer and also do some work in the 'outer' world. She said that once the writing vein was established, it would be possible to do both. She was right. By the time I found my room at Glenfern, I was able to combine my writing life with the planning and fundraising for the renovations, using skills I'd picked up in my earlier life. Fundraising was easier than writing; it took me back into 'left-brain' territory where I was comfortable. Now I had the perfect balance – solitude and writing for several days on end, interspersed with a project that involved working with others.

When I look back on my journey from the mid fifties to sixty, I see that I had to let go and allow my subconscious to lead me. I had to go into freefall, like a skydiver who plunges into the unknown for a while before opening his parachute and guiding himself towards a safe landing. As Peter O'Connor says in his book, *Facing the Fifties* – 'Doubt and uncertainty are part of the creative process.'

During this time I had to let go of a lot of things and mourn their losses. I had to face up to physical decline, to problems with hearing and eyesight, allergies and sleep disturbances. I had to spend more time keeping fit, with yoga and Pilates and exercise classes and regular walking.

I felt a loss of security and significance when I left my work in the 'outer' world for the uncertainty of the inner world. This was particularly confronting when I'd been part of the 'second wave' of feminism, the first generation to combine motherhood with a career and a role in the public domain. I was still interested in the world of politics and social issues, but I no longer wanted to work in it and that made me feel guilty. During the time that I was 'stuck' I felt that the best part of my life was over and it wouldn't matter if I died. I carried on with life as normal, but sometimes I was crying inside.

When I left the workforce, I wondered anxiously what to put on my business card. Then it dawned on me that my card didn't need to say anything at all, except my name and contact details. It was a liberating thought. Slowly I managed to throw overboard the excess baggage of titles, status, achievements and a male-dominated view of what was important in life.

During my journey to fifty and beyond I also had to face up to declining memory – of forgetting people's names and misplacing things and walking into a room and wondering what I'd gone in there for. The psychologist and author James Hillman says the older mind divides memories into 'short term' which fade, and 'long term' which improve. He says we spend more time doing a 'life review.' We commemorate moments which were of value and we depend less on other people for praise or recognition. We gain insight into our own character and draw conclusions from our past actions. Past struggles don't hurt as much and can even become amusing. He says the soul is letting go the weights it has been carrying.

That was certainly true for me. I was drawn irresistibly to writing about my past love affair because only by re-examining it in detail could I exorcise the anguish and bewilderment I'd felt at its ending. Dorothea Brande in her book *Becoming a writer*, says creativity comes from the memories and emotions of the past, which are stored in the unconscious. 'A sound person draws on these resources,' she says, 'not one who suppresses every echo from the far region at great cost to energy and vitality.'

Writing about the past helped me to understand for the first time why the various players in my small story had acted as they had, including myself. Reading my old letters and diaries allowed me to grieve all over again and finally to let go of anger and regret. The process of re-examining this story was cathartic and it enabled me to value all the more the life I'd built with Race and our love for each other.

The journey to sixty helped me to repair other relationships too, especially with my daughter and my brother and sister. Caring for my mother made me face up to her mortality and my own, but the antidote was the love and affection of my family and my new grandchild. I saw myself as being the fulcrum on a seesaw, with my mother at one end and my grandson at the other. She could pull me down, but he lifted me up.

Facing your own mortality has a comforting side – none of your petty concerns seem very important any more. When you see death ahead, or you attend the funeral of a friend, you feel an obligation to make the most of every minute left to you. The important thing is to move on, to try new things and not to be held back by fear.

By the time I turned sixty I was doing what I loved, and I knew that I would go on doing it for as long as I could think clearly and hold a laptop or pen and paper. It occurred to me that there should be a new word for 'retirement,' to reflect the fact that most of us can now enjoy twenty or even thirty years of active and liberated life after we leave the workplace. This 'third age' before you reach ill health and incapacity, is a bonus. You have more time for yourself, your partner and your friends. There is the joy of grandchildren. You have reached a time of maturity, of an acceptance of who you are.

But the path to this inner peace is not always easy. What matters is to live an authentic life, to have projects that interest you and to help others. As the writer Natalie Goldberg says in her book *Writing Down the Bones*, the important thing is to *'trust in what you love, continue to do it, and it will take you where you need to go.'*

---

1. The largest donor was the Pratt Foundation, which gave us $165,000 for the building and a further $10,000 for public events. The Victorian Government gave us $73,000 (from Arts Victoria and Heritage Victoria) and the rest came from the Helen Macpherson Smith Trust and the National Trust itself. More information about Glenfern is available from the Victorian Writers' Centre (www.vwc.org.au).